GW01066380

Sound Affects

Sado-Masochism and Sensation in Lars von Trier's *Breaking the Waves* and *Dancer in the Dark*

VDM Verlag Dr. Müller

Impressum/Imprint (nur für Deutschland/ only for Germany)

Bibliografische Information der Deutschen Nationalbibliothek: Die Deutsche Nationalbibliothek verzeichnet diese Publikation in der Deutschen Nationalbibliografie; detaillierte bibliografische Daten sind im Internet über http://dnb.d-nb.de abrufbar.

Alle in diesem Buch genannten Marken und Produktnamen unterliegen warenzeichen-, marken- oder patentrechtlichem Schutz bzw. sind Warenzeichen oder eingetragene Warenzeichen der jeweiligen Inhaber. Die Wiedergabe von Marken, Produktnamen, Gebrauchsnamen, Handelsnamen, Warenbezeichnungen u.s.w. in diesem Werk berechtigt auch ohne besondere Kennzeichnung nicht zu der Annahme, dass solche Namen im Sinne der Warenzeichen- und Markenschutzgesetzgebung als frei zu betrachten wären und daher von jedermann benutzt werden dürften.

Coverbild: www.purestockx.com

Verlag: VDM Verlag Dr. Müller Aktiengesellschaft & Co. KG
Dudweiler Landstr. 99, 66123 Saarbrücken, Deutschland
Telefon +49 681 9100-698, Telefax +49 681 9100-988, Email: info@vdm-verlag.de

Herstellung in Deutschland:
Schaltungsdienst Lange o.H.G., Berlin
Books on Demand GmbH, Norderstedt
Reha GmbH, Saarbrücken
Amazon Distribution GmbH, Leipzig
ISBN: 978-3-639-16349-0

Imprint (only for USA, GB)

Bibliographic information published by the Deutsche Nationalbibliothek: The Deutsche Nationalbibliothek lists this publication in the Deutsche Nationalbibliografie; detailed bibliographic data are available in the Internet at http://dnb.d-nb.de.

Any brand names and product names mentioned in this book are subject to trademark, brand or patent protection and are trademarks or registered trademarks of their respective holders. The use of brand names, product names, common names, trade names, product descriptions etc. even without a particular marking in this works is in no way to be construed to mean that such names may be regarded as unrestricted in respect of trademark and brand protection legislation and could thus be used by anyone.

Cover image: www.purestockx.com

Publisher:
VDM Verlag Dr. Müller Aktiengesellschaft & Co. KG
Dudweiler Landstr. 99, 66123 Saarbrücken, Germany
Phone +49 681 9100-698, Fax +49 681 9100-988, Email: info@vdm-verlag.de

Printed in the U.S.A.
Printed in the U.K. by (see last page)
ISBN: 978-3-639-16349-0

TABLE OF CONTENTS

People say that only they themselves can understand the pain they are feeling. But is this true? I for one do not believe that it is. If, before our eyes, we see someone who is truly suffering, we do sometimes feel his suffering and pain as our own. This is the power of empathy.

- Haruki Murakami

INTRODUCTION

Empathy and suffering. Two words which could effortlessly find their place in the cinematic lexicon prevalent in critical readings of the work of Danish director, Lars von Trier, whose films delve into themes of sacrifice and persecution in their desire to explore the sometimes darkened heart of human love and compassion. From *Breaking the Waves* in 1996, to *Mandalay* in 2005, von Trier's triptychs – the *Goldheart* cycle, and the *Americana* series (of which only the first two films are complete) – have been driven by female characters who are pushed to the very extremes of physical, emotional, and psychical endurance so that the limits of individual strength and spirit in their most translucently fragile states can be observed. An appreciation of these martyred women is central to the investigations of this project, which focuses on two of von Trier's films from this period: *Breaking the Waves* and *Dancer in the Dark* (2000). What is also of import are the auditory agents – both musical and spoken – at play in the narratives, and the manner in which they serve to make the thematics manifest and experienced by the spectator on a more direct and immediate level.

Derived from the German *einfühlung* or "in feeling… the power of identifying oneself mentally with (and so fully comprehending) a person or object of contemplation," (Barber) empathy is "one of the most important mechanisms through which we bridge the gap between experience and thought" (Szalita). In a clinical and/or therapeutic context, such identification, which extends beyond simple understanding, has been recognized as a central component in the rapport between doctor and patient, leading to greater success in the treatment of physiological and psychiatric illness. But what of the relationship that links the

3

people in the theatre with those up on the screen? Where does empathy locate itself, if at all, in the synthesis of identifications, subjectivities, and emotions which govern our responses when watching a film? And how might it be triggered?

When *Dancer in the Dark*, von Trier's reworking of the classic melodramatic and musical forms, was screened in Ontario, theatre owners were rumoured to have brought up the house lights immediately after the closing shot, rather than easing them on during the credit roll as was their standard practice. The motivation behind this unusual directive seemed resolute in its intentions: to return the audience from the dominion of the cinematic imaginary without delay so as to lessen the effect of the violent hanging death of the female protagonist. But such strategies had minimal impact on the viewers who surrounded me at my first screening of the film, and who wandered – alternately weeping or in stunned silence – into the lobby afterward.

I was among the inconsolable. My companion struggled to pull himself out of his own anesthetised stupor so as to better assume the role of care-giver, which was urgently needed as my sobbing had grown to encompass the totality of my physical being in its violent spasms. But such institutionalized gender distinctions, though perhaps productive in meditations on sexual difference and spectatorial position are beside the point here, as is a further elaboration of my anecdotal remembered experience which is necessarily rewritten in every moment that it comes to mind. What is of interest, however, are the questions these recollections posit on a film-theoretical level: how to articulate the cathartic physicality of the spectatorial response; how to best enunciate the signifying practices that contributed to its construction; and how to theorize the many pleasures it engendered. Was this an experience of empathy – an identification with suffering? Or was this simply suffering?

The distinctiveness and audacity of von Trier's oeuvre has garnered a substantial body of English-language analysis and criticism, most of which has appeared in the years following the release of *Breaking the Waves*, though there were several feature-length films, *The Kingdom* television series, and several short films which preceded it. These collections, which include Faber & Faber's popular *Directors on Directors* monograph, and the *Directors Series* from the British Film Institute, as well as a plethora of newspaper and journal reviews, can largely be divided into three categories: those that deal with von Trier's involvement in the *Dogme* 95 manifesto and its attendant attributes (Kelly); those that come from a more conventionally formalist or auteurist perspective (Björkman, Lumholdt, Stevenson); and those that engage in the nurturance and making of myth: extolling the virtues of this boldly talented wunderkind, or condemning his *enfant terrible* persona (Arroyo).

With this project, these more tangible interventions are balanced by an engagement with the texts that is deeply philosophical in nature. Here, an awareness of the receptive body adds *use-value* to the conceptual by grounding the theoretical in an accountable collective experience which extends far beyond my own. Bypassing examinations of von Trier as *Dogme* activist and/or persona, there is nevertheless an acknowledgement of his authorial station and the preoccupations which saturate his work: a fascination with cruelty and its effects on the female body – both latent and manifest. Of greater import, however, is an introduction to the philosophical framework upon which my thesis is built, and to the vocabulary critical to this unconventional approach to von Trier. Recognizing Gilles Deleuze's innovative typology of cinematic signs as the locus of contemporary scholarship on time and movement – as well as writing on sensation and affect – this project begins with Deleuze's cinema books, *The Movement-Image* and *The Time-Image*, seeking to articulate how his complementary construction of the filmic text informs my readings of the two films.

That von Trier's films are at the same time poignant, arousing and disturbing – that they seem to effect us *emotionally* – is what originally motivated this project and compelled me to seek perhaps unorthodox, or at least, counter-institutional theories of viewer response. But is it really on the level of emotion that we are engaging with these films? Here, I turn to the writings of Brian Massumi in *Parables for the Virtual*, and the distinction he draws between emotion, which is narrativizable and subjective, and only fully realized through the intrusions of conscious thought (28) – and affect, or *intensity*, which is "embodied in purely autonomic reactions… most directly manifested in the skin" (25). This notion of the viewing body as a *body* in its most literal and explicit sense, provides the basis for an inclusive analysis that acknowledges this corporeal spectator as one in a state of (always) becoming and who because of this, experiences the cinema most fully on a level that remains outside of intellectual thought.

The first film, *Breaking the Waves*, which despite its taxing subject matter, was nominated for an Academy Award, won the Palme D'Or at Cannes, and received wide-spread acclaim, depicts the "deceptively simple" story (Makarushka, 2) of Bess McNeil, a pious young woman whose religious purity and clarity of purpose contribute to her being dismissed by her sister-in-law, and some critics, as "not right in the head."[1] Such misunderstandings lend themselves to the perpetuation of this *deception* as Bess, under the ever-watchful but unseeing eyes of those who profess to love and care for her most, embarks on a journey of spiritual and sexual degradation that leads first to her expulsion from the church, and then to the unspeakable horrors of her torture and death. Alternately "transparent, cynical, hopeful, ironic, sincere, ugly, beautiful, and downright baffling," (Rosenbaum) the film has provoked countless responses, though my work moves away from strictly religious and/or formalist inquiry into questions involving the evocative correspondence of sado-masochism, modernity and music.

Here, what have historically been regarded as complementary phenomena within the psychology of sexual perversions – sadism and masochism – are dissected in dialogue with the filmic texts. What Bess (and later, Selma)[2] appear to share on the surface – although the reasons behind their abjection, and the character of their respective torments, are in each case different – is a tendency toward masochism and its essential behaviours that has seen von Trier's work cited in the company of Sade's. But this interpretation is problematic in its simplistic use of the lexis. Tracing these pathologies back to their literary roots, I return to Gilles Deleuze – whose study of Sacher-Masoch's *Venus in Furs* enables a recontextualization of *Breaking the Waves* within a newly-articulated sado-masochistic framework – before segueing into a discussion of the film's musical tropes.

Linking form to content, the film situates its eclectic use of sound in the character of Bess, who, like a turn-of-the-century *flâneuse* discovering the streets of the metropolis for the first time, makes her passage into modernity via the popular songs which usher in the exquisite landscapes of the chapter headings, and punctuate the many transgressions that drive her far from her emotional home. The visual polarities of these non-narrative segments and their narrative counterparts have been acknowledged in recent criticism (Makarushka, Rosenbaum); what has been lacking, however, is a meaningful discussion of the disparities in what is commonly known as the soundtrack.

In *Sound Theory/Sound Practice*, Rick Altman coins the expression *mise-en-bande* to facilitate a discourse on film sound that parallels that of the mise-en-scène, and to offer what is arguably a more effective term than *soundtrack*, which Michel Chion decries as "deceptive and sloppy... [for postulating that] the audio elements recorded together onto the optical track of the film are presented to the spectator as a sort of bloc or coalition" (1999: 3). This polemic is addressed as the nexus for an inquiry into music and voice that provides a structural link between the two films, and weaves the thematic and philosophical concerns of *Breaking the Waves* into the examination of *Dancer in the Dark* and its investigations into memory, genre, and the silencing of the female voice.

From the opening frames of *Dancer in the Dark*, something is clearly amiss. An image appears on the screen – layers of colours flickering almost into focus but never quite reaching clarity, the intimation of shapes shifting so as to never fully settle on that which is identifiable. Then the title card, hovering in space, unfixed and unsettling as though once again beheld by unsteady eyes. And from behind it, and present within the diegesis, random voices, and a decidedly recognizable song: "My Favourite Things" from *The Sound of Music*. In a matter of seconds, we are cued to the realization that we might embark on a different type of voyage, for *Dancer in the Dark* is about sightlessness, and a mode of knowledge which is heard rather than seen – an *audio-vision*.[3]

Considered in this context, Chion's provocation that "there is no soundtrack" (1999: 1) is difficult to refute because the disparate elements of the mise-en-bande are as distinct from their aural counterparts as the manifold visual constituents of the mise-en-scène. Here, Chion's *Audio-Vision* provides useful vocabulary for an enunciation of these various sounds, though his assertion that the cinema is essentially *vococentric*, that "the presence of a human voice structures the sonic space that contains it" is problematic, arguing for a new hierarchy in which "there are voices, and then everything else" (1995: 5). But, that a jazz drummer, for example, may foreground the rhythms of speech rather than its contents, works to counter this argument, as does the overt presence of popular music on both sides of the diegetic border – exposing the voice as just one component of a richly structured mise-en-bande, and drawing attention to the value of understanding how music also makes meaning in the cinematic text.

Acknowledging this theoretical obligation, I examine the ways in which *Dancer in the Dark* (and *Breaking the Waves*) concretize themes of transcendental communion and divine insight through their treatment of music and voice: in Bess, a diegetic conduit who enacts the desires of an almighty off-screen presence – what Chion marks as an *acousmêtre* or "voice without a place" (1999: 27) – and in Selma, a *hearer* of songs who finds herself in transtextual communication with a music generated outside the diegesis. That both women inhabit a space where fantasy and reality intersect without clearly defined boundaries, posits their experiential position as analogous to that of the spectator, and resembling them: "we too are led into dreaming with our eyes open" (Studlar, 28). But while this statement resonates on one level, a closer look at Studlar's language – this idea of being led – is revealed as problematic for its allegiance to a particular strain of psychoanalytic film theory external to the focus of this project. Could a new approach lie instead in the notion of *our* having fallen into the gap that exists between these two *space-times* – the fantastic and the concrete, the time-image and the movement-image, the masochistic and the sadistic – and that it is in this gap, this fleeting moment, between "*content* and *effect*" (Massumi, 24) that we not only discover the possibility of affect, but experience it?

When screening *Dancer in the Dark* a second time as research for this thesis, I was curious as to how the aforesaid climactic scene would impact me – having seen the film, and having become familiar with its narrative trajectory. Sitting alone, watching on a computer monitor with a headset blocking out distractions, I was confident that my reaction would be less severe, and as the plot wound toward its inevitable finale, any anxiety I might have otherwise experienced was lessened by rational thought as I divided my focus between the screen and my notes. Still, when the noose snapped in mid-phrase and sent Selma to her soundless death, I felt once again as though I had been physically struck, and swallowed the urge to cry out, to shatter this oppressive silence. That the film could sustain this power, despite the critical distance created by the academic nature of my engagement and my conscious efforts to remain detached, was instructive. This was not empathy, not an identification with suffering – this was suffering.

This return to the words of Haruki Murakami reminds us again of our two central heroines: Bess, and Selma – the awkward waif-like creature in coke-bottle glasses whose presence is made all the more astonishing by the film's utter disregard for the tropes of the conventional heroine. Acting in accordance with a complicated worldview inherited (via *Idioterne*'s Karen)[4] from Bess, Selma sustains a moral certainty that is grounded in the knowledge that "to live outside the law is to live in exile from the communities of humanity" (Carter, 41). In interviews, von Trier has compared Bess to the character of *Goldheart* herself, the young protagonist of his favourite childhood fable about a girl who sets out for a picnic in the forest, but suffers many travails and ends up naked and alone. That the character, despite her misfortunes, possesses the spiritual fortitude to end the story with the statement, "at least I'm okay," communicates the "ultimate extremity of the martyr's role" (Björkman, 164). But Bess and Selma are not okay, and it is in his attempts to articulate this

8

altruism cinematically that von Trier's most zealous detractors locate their hostility, seeing only "cynicism and a shameless crudity" (Rosenbaum) from a "misanthropic bully" (Edelstein) whose notion of women as "self-sacrificing saintly whores" is nothing more than a "flimsy illusion of profundity" (Turan).

That von Trier's harshest critics – at least in the reviews amassed here – are men is somewhat surprising in light of the films' graphic depictions of female persecution and suffering. Is there something fundamental in the experience of a "woman martyrised by the circumstances of her life as a woman" (Carter, 38) that women are more capable of identifying with, or is it an inherent understanding of a "love so strong that it removes any sense of self-preservation" (Arpe) that makes the films more palatable to female viewers? Perhaps it is due to the fact that Bess, like Selma, is not merely a "woman in a man's world; she is also a receptacle of feeling, a repository of the type of sensibility we call *feminine*" (Carter, 47). But despite this receptivity, these women cannot withstand the sadistic brutality of the texts in which they exist, transformed in the moment from a body into a *body-without-organs*,[5] "distraught and disconnected," (Massumi, 106) the mute vessels through which the reverberations of *Breaking the Waves* and *Dancer in the Dark* are received by the spectator as "pure sensation" (109).

For in each of these two films, we are made witness to something utterly new – an *any-space-whatever* that exists *between* the real and the fantastic; the "point of transit between places of importance... the space one passes through... depersonalized" (Totaro).[6] Here, in the *any-space-whatevers* that exist both within and around these two narratives, the affective moment – whether experienced in the short, sharp blow of *Dancer in the Dark*'s concluding scene, or sustained, as it is at the end of *Breaking the Waves* – offers a spectatorial experience that is distinct. Like the enslaved lover whose cruel mistress taunts and teases until he must beg and plead for climactic release, we too are held captive in a state of eternal becoming by a pair of texts whose affective authority leaves us powerless to overcome the body, despite our efforts to engage on the level of an emotional, empathic understanding.

Exciting is the fact that these new and sometimes contentious modalities of thinking on sensation and affect are still in their relative infancy, and so are operating in an imprecise space lacking the rigorous consideration paid to the canonic texts on spectatorship from the seventies and eighties. There is, however, much that is meaningful here, as film studies is presented with an opportunity for contributions to the discourse from outside the canon, and innovative approaches to von Trier's cinematic corpus.

I feel a lot of sympathy for humanists and all the humiliations they have to suffer. At the same time, I don't think it's unreasonable that they have to suffer the things that they have to go through... humanism is based on a fairly naïve concept. I still think humanism is a good basis for possible co-operation here on Earth. But there is a lot of fiction in humanism. The idea that people will take the trouble to co-operate and work for the good of their fellow man is deeply naïve.

- Lars von Trier[7]

CHAPTER ONE

Reading Lars von Trier through Gilles Deleuze

Suffering. Not empathy. Affect. Not emotion. But is this merely a game of semantics, of word play? And if so, what is its purpose? In many ways, this project's preoccupations have always extended beyond the realm of cinematic enquiry to thinking about the relationship between feeling and thought. Habitually polemicized as dichotomic in character, this intangible pairing (and its tensions) finds numerous manifestations in the two texts: *Breaking the Waves* and *Dancer in the Dark*. That these doubled structures and thematic couplets – good and evil, man and woman, sound and vision, masochism and sadism – dominate in the films is clear. What is less evident, however, is how these seemingly oppositional facets of human experience can be best understood within the context of spectatorial response, and which of the monolithic film theories is best-suited to the task of articulating these dualisms and the effects they hold for the viewer. The answer is none. In fact, this line of thinking moves in the wrong direction. Instead, we must diverge from those approaches that seek to sustain this dichotomy and reposition these dyadic relationships as complementary. Hence I turn to the writings of Gilles Deleuze, and to a different way of working cinematically – to a philosophy of the cinema that argues against this polemic, reconstructing the image as containing two relational semiotics:[8] one of time and one of movement, the crystalline and the organic, the abstract and the empathic.[9]

The arm of philosophy that traces its lineage backward from Descartes through to Plato has been seen as a quest for what might be described as a sort of elemental truth, a pre-existent knowledge to be divined or parsed, rather than as the creation of an object for contemplation. As von Trier confirms in the quotation that begins this chapter, there is also a tendency to evaluate philosophy on the basis of a practicable application, an activity in which it seems almost certain to fail, or at least, to falter; as the collision between the conceptual and human nature often proves too volatile for the action to be sustained over time.[10] Thus, despite our desire that it may do so, philosophy cannot protect us from suffering. Instead, we must recognize it as a "practice... [to] be judged in light of the other practices with which it interferes..." because it is through these *interferences* that "things happen, beings, concepts, all the kinds of events" (Deleuze, 1989: 280). The central idea here is *creation*, as the constructivist empiricism of Deleuze (and Félix Guattari)[11] proffers an understanding of philosophy as the art of "forming, inventing, and fabricating concepts" (Deleuze and Guattari, 1994: 2). This innovative approach, when practiced in dialogue with the cinematic texts, rallies against more conventional interpretive modalities of analysis such as hermeneutics – with its "*always already...* truth that remains to be discovered" (Flaxman, 3) – and so its consideration for inclusion into the canon of film studies has been contentious. Yet it is precisely this capacity for *creating* with concepts, images, and in particular, *sound-images*, that attracted me to this constructivist methodology. And so the cinema of Lars von Trier collides with the philosophies of Gilles Deleuze, and in this moment, is reread and rewritten, creating new objects for enunciation.

Speaking with American director P.T. Anderson in 2004, von Trier conceded that it is "very easy to invent new things all the time, but... not very mature," stating that if he "meant something" with his films, he should "underline it by going on [with the same]" (Black, 3). On a thematic level, certainly, there is a unity that transcends the more overt machinations of style across the corpus; a coherence most clearly read through the films' focal characters. But before introducing a discussion of the heroines and their respective partners, it is necessary to examine the formal conceits that unite *Breaking the Waves* and *Dancer in the Dark*.[12]

As mentioned in the introduction, von Trier's feature films are grouped into three visually and thematically distinct trilogies: *Europa* (1984-91) is an oppressively stylized exercise that explores the woes of a "Europe that has been lulled to sleep in the midst of its own chaos and death" (Belzer); the *Goldheart* trilogy (1996-2003) investigates the notion of goodness with a relentless hand-held camera and penchant for extreme close-ups; while the *Americana* series (2003-05)[13] with its questionable politics and naïve reading of America's social history, takes its formal cues from Peter Watkin's *La Commune*, setting its narratives in a vague and cartoonishly-delineated mise-en-scène. Because of the explicit stylistic coherences found within these triadic cycles, it seems logical for this thesis to have dealt exclusively with just one of these self-contained filmic units, but there is a third, more salient level of address that motivated my selection of films: the affective implications of their respective mise-en-bandes.

Much has been made of the affective qualities of the mise-en-scène, especially in the genre of horror,[14] but less attention has been given to the arena of sound. To listen to *Dancer in the Dark* with the picture absent is to experience the work from an entirely different level of perception in which the heretofore accepted hierarchy of vision over sound is no longer supreme. This can also be said of the other text, and perhaps, of sound film in general – though this argument may seem counter-intuitive to adherents of a more formalist ocular-centric practice that continues to privilege vision as "the basis for engagement" (Buhler, 73). In her monograph, *Unheard Melodies*, Claudia Gorbman, Michel Chion's colleague and translator, posits that the spectator can no longer consider music – and I would argue, all the types of sounds that are produced outside the diegetic space[15] – as merely "incidental or innocent" (11). I wholeheartedly agree. Sound must be released from its subordination to the image, and recognized as having an independence that allows it to provoke, seduce, and make meaning in collusion with its visual counterparts. And while the mise-en-bande may never achieve the degree of autonomy granted to the mise-en-scène,[16] it must be read (again) as complementary rather than subservient, and one whose level of engagement can be read as *infra-sensorial*; with vision as just one of the manifold senses. A comprehensive discussion of sound and its affective properties is developed in the following chapters, but it is crucial that a few of the basic conceits upon which this argument is predicated are made manifest here.

First, a note on the terminology. When film studies speaks of form, we presume to be talking about the visual domain and its stylistic qualities (again, with the tacit agreement that film style is semantically interchangeable with visual style). This is second nature, but this must change. Instead, we must assign the elements of the mise-en-bande a direct correspondence to those found in the mise-en-scène, acknowledging them as intrinsic components of the cinema's overall formal structure. An acceptance of this proposition is essential to my arguments, and so I submit this model for consideration: the *image*, that is to say, the thing that is "preserved... [the] bloc of sensations, of percepts and affects" (Deleuze and Guattari, 1994: 164) should be recognized as the visual complement to what we might call the *sound-image*.[17]

Here, Deleuze and Guattari's use of the provocatively vague (and admittedly preposterous) *thing* – which they use in reference to a single work of art – turns out to be wonderfully liberating because it is blissfully free from the signifying baggage of any identifiable film-theoretical and/or historical tradition. The *shot*, on the other hand, is not so lucky, and so we witness Michel Chion grappling with its determinates as he seeks to employ it in the context of his theorizing on sound.[18] In light of this dilemma, I prefer to think the sound-image as quite simply a *thing* that in its resistance to unnecessary categorization or naming, can simply be what it is: a musical phrase, a sudden crash, an utter silence... a *sensation*, a *percept*, an *affect*. This moves the project forward, yet my work is not quite complete. Now that I have mapped out this paradigm, I must extend the correspondence. What follows is by necessity an over-simplification of the concepts created in Deleuze's *Cinema* books. That said, it is sufficient to the task of elucidating his dyadic construction of the cinema that identifies the image (and therefore, the sound-image) as one of movement (*movement-sound*) or time (*time-sound*).

In essence, what Deleuze has done is divide film history into two distinct phases: that which precedes World War II, and that which follows. The pre-war cinema, a cinema that for the most part includes both the era of silent film, and that of the early sound narratives, is characterized, according to Deleuze, as a cinema of movement. By this, Deleuze means a cinema in which time is subordinate to movement, a cinema that is causal, in which a series of *movement-images*, each with a comprehensible relationship to that which came before it and that which follows, are read as movement. This, despite the fact that there is no *real* movement in the cinema; all movement is *false* – a perceptual illusion created through the trickery of editing (Deleuze, 1986: 2) Though Deleuze's departure point is different from narrative, in layman's terms, we can understand these movement-images as just that, images from which the narrative is constructed.[19] We can also situate the mise-en-bande in this context, for the movement-sound, that which we might (for the sake of ease and clarity) conceptualize as a synchronous, diegetic, and *natural* sound, most often embodied in the human voice "imposes on the [visual] sequence as a sense of real time" (Chion, 1994: 16).[20]

Because of this, both the movement-image and the movement-sound can be seen as working in tandem to create an *organic* regime, organic because "the real that is assumed is recognizable by its continuity... it is a regime of localizable relations, actual linkages, legal, causal, and logical connections" (Deleuze, 1989: 126-127). It is also a regime that comforts, at least in the sense that comfort may be born of the certainty inherent in these linkages and continuities, leading to a "harmonious unity where humanity feels at one with the world" (Rodowick, from Worringer, 8). Since the movement-image creates opportunities for this level of emotional engagement, it can also be understood as that which opens the door to the possibility of empathic response.[21]

Wilhelm Worringer, whose work in turn pays enormous debt to Theodor Lipps' *Aesthetik*, is also key to this discourse. Written in the early years of the last century, his book *Abstraction and Empathy* argues for a new approach to the study of aesthetics, especially in relation to what is sometimes labelled the *plastic* arts. In this text, Worringer entreats us to reconsider the relationship between the art object and its viewer, because the art-theoretical tradition up to the point of his writing had derived almost exclusively from a theory of empathic response that excluded "wide tracts of art history" (4). In arguing his hypothesis, Worringer delineates a clear division between *positive* empathy – in which the giving of oneself over to "the activity demanded... without opposition, [engenders] a feeling of liberty... of pleasure" – and its *negative* complement. In the latter, the conflict that arises between the "natural striving for self-activation and the one that is demanded [by the object] leads to sensations of *unpleasure* (6). These definitions will come into greater play in the analytical chapters, but for now, allow us to develop a more *geometric* sense of what the empathic plane of the binary-chain represents: the movement-image, the movement-sound, and as I will argue, the sadistic character sustained by the structures of the organic regime.[22]

Accusations of a different type of sadism endure in the critical response to von Trier's work, and in assessments of his directorial strategies. Labels such as misogynist and misanthrope proliferate in these texts as von Trier, in film after film, "nails another heroine to the cross" (Wilmington). But what of these heroines? Comparable perhaps to Hitchcock's much-enunciated fascination with the "cool blonde beauty" (Gopnik, 44) of the Grace Kelly/Kim Novak/Tippi Hedren triad, von Trier's unwavering devotion to an explicitly good

15

and self-sacrificing woman (though his choice of actors is notable for their lack of discernible physical similarities) suggests that "death can be overcome, or at least made tolerable, by repetitive obsessions" (47).[23]

With Björk as Selma in *Dancer in the Dark*, and Emily Watson as *Breaking the Waves'* Bess McNeil, there also exists two actors who not only took on the challenge of embodying this archetype of female suffering, but did so at the hands of this infamously demanding *master* who "like the father in the sadistic scenario... playacts at liberating women" (Studlar, 20) but ultimately demands their absolute submission to the role; their performative subordination a symbolic act of "ordered negation" (21). Björk promotes this assessment, suggesting that von Trier "needs a female to provide his work [with] soul... envies them and hates them for it, [and] so has to destroy them during filming" (Björk).[24] And while this allegation may be difficult to confirm, von Trier's admission to Paul Thomas Anderson in a later discussion about *Dogville*'s lead actor is telling: "I liked Nicole very much, or anyway, I liked her character" (*Black*, 2). This glimpse behind the scenes helps contextualize our understanding of the female characters, but it is of equal import to introduce the men – for in both instances, this archetypical male (some would say surrogate, but we will get to this later) plays a crucial, ultimately antagonistic role that is central to the trajectory of these martyred women; a complementary dyad that is as relevant to our investigation as that of the relationship between the movement-image and the time-image.

Portrayed as learned – either by book, or through an engagement with the world that lies beyond the reach of their female counterparts – these men identify themselves as both morally and intellectually superior to the women in their lives. Yet, the ostensible sophistication of *Breaking the Waves'* Jan, and *Dancer in the Dark*'s Bill, is only fully perceptible in contrast to the almost primitive intellects of everyone around them, and does not immunize them from emotional torment, despite the emphasis the film consigns to the suffering of the female leads. Even as their brutally misguided ideas are made real, their collective inability to grasp the consequences of their actions reveals them as too dense to be truly culpable. As events transpire, the heretofore unchallenged authority of the hero's *knowledge* is confronted by the divine wisdom of the emblematic heroine, his idealism dismantled by the almost spiritual pragmatism of her convictions. Yet this does not prevent him from plunging head-first into the encroaching darkness of his imagined universe, as though convinced that in his attempt to enact a belief system, he will achieve the sort of moral salvation that can only be delivered at the hand of his hallowed other. And while the relationships diverge – husband/wife, father-figure/innocent – this same battle plays itself out in both Jan and Bill, though it is the former who remains the most explicit manifestation of the struggle to *live* philosophy.

That these men – for whom the narrative acts as a sadistic master (an idea that will be discussed in greater detail in the next chapter) – are led into these circumstances by forces just beyond their control does not excuse their actions, but does go some way to explain the rationalizations behind their decisions, at least in moments of private communion. As they seek deliverance from a world whose controlling structures seem committed to breaking their spirit, an offer of redemption appears from an unlikely source: the women, whose moral convictions are so complicated that they somehow manage to justify unthinkable sacrifice as an act of compassion and redemption. To take a step back from the filmic texts, the question now becomes this: how do we, as the audience, characterize our response to this narrative construct – is it an experience of pleasure or unpleasure; an activity of self-activation or self-alienation?

For Worringer, the instinct for self-alienation, is an "urge to abstraction [that is] the outcome of a great inner unrest inspired in man by the phenomena of the outside world" (Worringer, 15). This is where the political manifests, in a "will to power... the power of creation, where the values... are not principles for thinking, but examples of that which has not yet been thought" (Rodowick, 138). Worringer describes this state as "an immense spiritual dread of space" (15). We might also portray it as the crystalline – the regime that finds its manifestation in a post-war cinema, the cinema of time.

Deleuze's *time-image* (which is infinitely richer in complexity and has resonated more vigorously among contemporary scholars) is understood to subvert the dominion of movement. Here, "time ceases to be the measurement of normal movement, it... appears for itself and creates paradoxical movements" (Deleuze, 1989: xi). To put it plainly, the time-image *creates* time because it exists outside of causality; drawing us away from the narrative and leaving us, if only for a moment, to our own devices. The time-sound can be said to function in the same manner. Proffered here as those sounds produced outside of the diegesis, the time-sound can be musical, spoken, or mechanical. It can also be silent. But regardless of which form it takes, its primary attribute remains its disconnect from any line of causality. This can be unsettling for the viewer. In a cinema constructed entirely of time-images, such as those existing within the realm of experimental film, we are prepared for this insecurity. These films require a different level of engagement and we come to them with the knowledge that we are going to be doing much of the work on our own – a proposition seen as undesirable by the genre's detractors. But the spectator's task becomes particularly exigent when the cinema is constructed out of both movement-images and time-images, especially when the time-images are behaving in a duplicitous fashion.

Take *Caché* from 2006, Michael Haneke's masterful exploration into race, class, and bourgeois paranoia in contemporary Paris. This film stumped audience members and critics alike because its ending was so obtuse that viewers were left with the distinct feeling that they had somehow missed something. Even viewers, who prompted by critics, had arrived with an especially conscious gaze were stymied. Theatres were difficult to clear as audiences sat puzzled in their chairs, wondering what had just happened to them; what had happened to the narrative closure they had come to expect. For weeks, critics grappled with solutions, seeking enlightenment in myriad possible explanations, but few were satisfying. Then it dawned on me – this was, by all surface appearances a narrative constructed, as Deleuze would say, from movement-images, whereas in truth, the film was built out of time-images that were merely posing as movement-images, and because of this, there was no possibility for *resolution*.[25]

As mentioned earlier, this *uncertainty* that Deleuze elucidates carries political overtones as well, for the simple reason that the time-image "[brings] into question the notion of truth" and in doing so, moves "beyond the true or the false" (Deleuze, 1989: 275). For now, however, it is important to illuminate the concept of the crystal, because it is in this crystalline regime that the true nature of the time-image is best understood. One of the defining characteristics of a crystal is that within its form is a multitude of planar surfaces. These planes allow for a refraction of light that gives the crystal the appearance of having not only multiple surfaces, but multiple dimensions that are produced internally through the act of manifold divisions. In the same way, the time-image can be understood as a crystalline image because within it, "the past is constituted not after the present that it was, but at the same time, has to split itself in two at each moment as present and past" (Deleuze, 1989: 81). In other words, the uncertainty of the crystalline regime produces an interval that becomes "what probability physics calls a *bifurcation point*, where it is impossible to know or predict in advance which direction change will take" (Rodowick, 15). Hence, with a time-image, the interval "is not the link bridging images, but rather the interstice between them, an unbridgeable gap which recurs endlessly [and through which,] identity and totality [are] no longer possible" (Manning). And if identification, with its obvious subjectivities, is no longer possible, what remains is the collective. In these time-images, we step outside ourselves, leaving room for that which is only possible on the collective level: affect.

Up to this point, Deleuze's arguments have made perfect sense. The distinctions between the movement-image and the time-image are logical and coherent, but when one starts to work with them, they can bog down in seemingly contradictory and certainly confusing ways. For though the time-image and the movement-image may seem oppositional, in truth, they are not. So where does this leave us?

Since the onset of auteur theory in the fifties, critics have debated the concept of film authorship, a polemic which came to its first head with Roland Barthes' declaration that the "birth of the reader must be at the cost of the Author," (1977) and continues to impact hermeneutic and semiotic scholarship with its questions of influence and intent. In a review of *Breaking the Waves* in *Slate Magazine*, Sarah Kerr seeks an explanation (or perhaps, justification) for her ambivalence as a spectator, using von Trier's words as evidence in her case against this "attractive manipulator [who] seems to know all about love, but... turns out to know only what works" (Kerr). Citing an interview von Trier gave to *The New York Times* earlier that year, she volunteers the following quote: "I was a projectionist and I was always watching the audience – that's how I know what works" (Kerr, from von Trier). However, in using this confession to explain why the film fails (or alternately, succeeds) to be more profound, Kerr is not only ascribing too much authorial control to von Trier, but is assigning so much weight to her own individual identifications and subjectivities that she completely dispenses with the experience of the collective.

Deleuze and Guattari would agree, because for them, the film (or any work of art) is a "self-positing of the created" that is independent of not only its model, but of the viewer and the creator as well (1994: 163-164). In this line of thinking, the work of art is able to "stand up on its own" not *because* of any inherent knowledge or divined instinct on the part of the creator, but for the simple reason that the "compound of created sensation is preserved in itself... solid and lasting" (1994: 164-165). Yet, having arrived at this conclusion in 1991,[26] in earlier works, such as the *Cinema* books, Deleuze exhibits a tendency toward the auteurist tradition that some critics have found quite tedious. In his introduction to *Gilles Deleuze's*

Time Machine, author David Rodowick says that "Deleuze's problematic attitude toward film authorship represents one of the worst aspects of Parisian cinephilism" (xiv). This is just one of the aspects of Deleuze's work that Rodowick finds *indefensible*, though he chooses to focus his monograph on that which he cites as *original* and *consistent* in the text's philosophical arguments (xv). And indeed there is something incongruous in the pairing of such obtuse theorizing with the kind of fandom associated with more formalist traditions. But, at the same time, it is refreshing to be able to engage with a practice that is deeply philosophical without having to apologize for an appreciation of the cinematic form and its *masters.*[27]

Perhaps the easiest way to reconcile these tensions is to return to the later text. Here, Deleuze and Guattari speak of the *artist*, who regardless of his chosen medium, is responsible for the presentation "of affects... they not only create them in their work, they give them to us and make us become with them, they draw us in (1994: 175). And as the work of Deleuzian scholars suggests, this is what is most profitable in his writings. He borrows, and transforms, and so do we. For me, working with Deleuze necessitates a bringing of the theoretical into the realm of my own physical language – personal and concrete. This is what I have done in trying to create workable concepts for the movement-sound and the time-sound, however imperfect they may be. At the very least, they are granted the freedom to grow and transform (and perhaps even, to contradict) as they adapt to the ideas and contexts encountered during the analytical process. Because of this, they enable a dialogue with the cinematic texts that is itself an act of becoming in which new readings and new understandings of von Trier's work are created. The final task then, before moving into these analyses, is to address one of the lingering incongruities in the *Cinema* books: that of the affection-image. Though in order to fully address this typological conundrum, we must quickly preface the work of Brian Massumi and his *Parables for the Virtual* so as to establish an awareness of what we are really talking about when we talk about affect.

As I mentioned in the introduction, Massumi is engaged in a project that while not specifically geared to the study of cinema, provides a lucid articulation of what is essentially a straightforward proposition: that the body, as an organ of sensation, is transformed through its "interface with things," (25) and that this transformation can be best understood not as a means to an end, but as a process – an ontology of *becoming* rather than *being*. This is an important distinction, and there are others. For Massumi, the fact that affect "is most often used… as a synonym for emotion" is problematic, and he argues compellingly for a clear delineation of the two (27). He is right to do so. The trouble with reading the affective and the emotional as equivalents, is that the latter requires thought. However, for thought to occur, time (and movement) must halt. And when movement halts, there is being. This is not affect, and this is not becoming. This is what we have come to understand as the movement-image. And so we arrive at the only seemingly reasonable conclusion available: that the relationship between the time-image and the affective experience is direct and incontrovertible: but this is far from the truth.

What makes the affection-image so outwardly problematic is that it is both a movement-image and a time-image. But how can this be? This confusion becomes even more tangible if we accept the equation proffered above: that the movement-image is an empathic image precisely because it suspends time, thereby producing an instance of *being* (however infinitesimal) during which thought (and therefore, empathy) occurs. But is this an accurate assessment? Not completely. What is of greater value in trying to coming to terms with this paradoxical construct is to look beyond the images themselves to that which occurs on the bridge between them. As stated earlier, movement-images are connected to other movement-images by linkages that *bridge* the gaps along the causal chain, and in doing so, create the (false) movement inherent to the organic regime. Whether manifested as hard edits, slow fades, or dissolves, when we travel across these bridges, each new cut compels the viewer to reconcile themselves to a new, albeit continuous, space-time. In these moments, the viewer becomes ensnared: we rest, we think, we are. Needless to say, this process transpires in the unconscious realm, as the façade of movement is forever sustained as unbroken along its surface; but it is there, nonetheless. That said, as a viewer, we are still *becoming* bodies – this has not changed. Despite having to *be* and *think*, we are still being forced by the cinema to fundamentally alter our modes of perception.

The time-image, on the other hand, does not suspend time or movement, because in the creation of its new space-time, it sends movement in new directions, thereby opening a gap or *interval* where the bridge of the movement-image would normally be. Here, the interval "no longer forms part of the image or sequence as the ending of one or the beginning of the other" – instead it is autonomous; what Deleuze would label "irrational" (Rodowick, 13-14). In the case of an otherwise narrative film, the viewer, unprepared for this interval, is caught in a free fall that causes the linearity of the organic regime to splinter into the crystalline. This creates an affective experience which is beyond description; it cannot be named or defined, and because of this, cannot be solved or put away. There is no place to locate it. It is outside of thought.

Yet, as has been discussed, these are not oppositional concepts. In actuality, thought may occur in the time-image, but it is what Deleuze would call *incommensurable* – freed from the insistent forwardness of the movement-image to wander, meditate, luxuriate. By the same token, the reversal of this equation also stands true; there is an opportunity for affect within the organic regime. This is the *affection-image*. Described as an *avatar* of the movement-image, the affection-image occurs when "within one image an interval is opened as a movement received on one side and as a movement executed on the other" (Rodowick, 57). In other words, in the interval between the *perception-image* (or object) and the *action-image* (its external response) – the affection-image is what allows the object to feel itself "from the inside" (Deleuze, 1986: 65). That this avatar, which for Deleuze is most visibly present in the close-up of an expressive face, locates itself in the interval, is what affirms its correspondence to the time-image. In more traditional cinematic terms, the close-up functions as an affection-image because it is a literal representation of this interval between the object and its response, cutting-away from the continuous movement of the wider-shot (perception) and then returning to it afterward (action).

On the level of the mise-en-bande, we might think of the *affection-sound* as having three possible manifestations: in on-screen voices that engage in transtextual communication, speaking or singing without the presence of a diegetic listener; in whispered on-screen voices in close-up that while participating in dialogue with individuals within the diegesis, nonetheless speak (or sing) as though directly into the viewer's ear, thereby breaking down what reflexive cinema refers to as the fourth wall; and in the diegetic silences that accompany the responsive face in close-up. That these decontextualized images cause the type of splintering or fragmentation of linearity that we have come to expect from the time-image, and thus create an experiential moment within the interval, is what enables us to align their outcomes with that of affect.

This may not wholly reconcile the tensions in Deleuze's *Cinema* books, but there is really no need to do so. Instead, we must hold ourselves back from such compulsions. As Deleuze and Guattari assert: "philosophy is becoming, not history... that which must be thought and that which cannot be thought" (1994: 59) – a process of creation that asks us to

22

play by those rules of engagement. The task of the philosopher then is to "no longer accept concepts as a gift, nor merely purify or polish them, but first to *make* and *create* them, present them, and make them convincing" (from Nietzsche, 1994: 5).

As has been made clear, there are numerous dyadic complements that come into play in the reading of these two films – too many to include them all here. That said, as we move into the analyses, it is imperative that my methodology for approaching the films is transparent and coherent. The diagram below illustrates the key complements and relationships along the binary-chain. On the top row, the plane of the movement- image (and

movement	thought	organic	empathic	subjective
↕	↕	↕	↕	↕
time	feeling	crystalline	affective	collective

movement-sound), thought is produced through an organic regime that is conveyed as a highly subjective, empathic (and emotional) response. The bottom row, on the other hand, brings to light a completely different phenomenon. Here, on the plane of the time-image (and time-sound), feeling is marshalled through a crystalline regime that results in the experience of collective affect. But how can these terms be effectively integrated into the analyses of the texts?

For me, water provides the most useful imagery when trying to visualize and articulate these two planes. The causality of the organic regime surges like a tributary: sometimes as slow and meandering as the Mississippi, and other times, crashing along like the white-water rivers of the Rocky Mountains. The crystalline is also part of this water system, but can be understood as having the same qualities as a swirling eddy. It pulls us away from the river's course and suspends us temporarily until the force of the current tugs us back into its flow. And in the ephemeral inbetween, in the moment of release, this *any-space-whatever*, is where we finally locate the root of our suffering for it is here that we are made most vulnerable by the affect of the time-image, and from here that we are thrust back into the often unpleasant – and in the case of Lars von Trier, emotionally agonizing – trajectory of the movement-image's empathic plane.

Thus we arrive at the end of this chapter with a greater understanding of Deleuze and his cinematic typology, but this is just the beginning. What lies at the heart of this thesis is a desire to explore the affective correspondence between sound and sado-masochism. And so to *Breaking the Waves*.

Everyday I spend my time, drinking wine, feeling fine
waiting here to find the sign that I can understand, yes I am.
In the days between the hours, ivory towers, bloody flowers,
Push their heads into the air, I don't care if I ever know, there I go.
Don't push your love too far...

- David Bentley[28]

CHAPTER TWO

Breaking the Waves: Music, Modernity and the Sado-Masochistic Entity

Despite its pervasiveness in contemporary pop-cultural discourse, the notion of a sado-masochistic entity is highly problematic in its assumption that a mutually beneficial relationship exists between the sadist and the masochist, for no such pairing can satisfy in actual practice. To put it simply, and in admittedly generalized terms, the sadist gains no gratification in extracting pain from a willing victim, and the masochist does not engage in play[29] with a master whom they cannot choose, and to some extent, control. Still, it is difficult to speak of one without the other as in each of their manifold behaviours there is a "meeting of violence and sexuality" which locates its origin in the "abundant language" of the Marquis de Sade, and Leopold von Sacher-Masoch, respectively (Deleuze, 1971: 17). Working from a comparative account of the authors' texts, this chapter builds upon the thematic framework introduced earlier, raises questions for immediate (and later) address, and submits a reading of *Breaking the Waves* that seeks to better understand the characters of Bess and Jan, recontextualizing their relationship within the arena of music and voice.

We begin with that same hovering title card from *Dancer in the Dark*, but here it reads: *Breaking the Waves*. It flickers on screen for no more than a second or two. Behind it, and again within the diegetic space, the reverberations of wind gusting across a vast and barren shoreline, and captured by an invisible microphone whose presence is nonetheless felt, saturating our impressions with its evocation of salt water and bracing cold. There is no music here, no melodramatic swell of strings to set the emotional tone, only the stark isolation of an aural landscape devoid of human resonance. Then suddenly, there is Bess. She appears first in extreme close-up, an unfamiliar face made even more foreign, her features made imprecise by the coarse grains of the 35mm print – a textbook example of an affection-image. Here, we have just begun our forward trajectory into the narrative when we are suddenly dropped into the interval that the affection-image produces. For a moment we hang there, as though suspended, until the next movement-image picks us up and carries us back downstream. Her eyes explore the perimeters of the frame, always watchful and alert, drinking in her surroundings with the curiosity of a small child whose pre-linguistic ability to interact with its world depends on the collusion of its five senses.[30] This is not a purely visual introduction, however, for speech is also present in this first moment, a rich musical brogue whose existence surprises long into the film – like the impossible voice of a mute, it seems channelled, rather than spoken, from deep within her soul.

The opening sequence is only one minute and thirty-seven seconds in duration, delivering us into the narrative on a burst of fresh air. In a succession of jump-cuts, Bess converses with a chorus of humourless clergymen on the subject of her intended, a brawny Swede named Jan who works on the rigs. Fearful of allowing an outsider to sully the purity of their strict Calvinist community, the men ask her to name one thing of "real value that the outsiders have brought with them." There is no hesitation in her response: "their music." She is sent from the church so the elders can ruminate without interruption. Once outside, the wind is reunited with its synchronous source, and Bess, transcending spoken language, looks directly at the camera and smiles, an intimation of suppressed agency conveyed by a knowing glance. With an abrupt cut to the first non-narrative chapter heading (which we can now identify as a time-image) made all the more striking by the sudden arrival of Mott the Hoople's glam-rock anthem "All the Way from Memphis" on the mise-en-bande (the time-sound), we are plunged into the film proper, and into the heart of this investigation.

In *Masochism: An Interpretation of Coldness and Cruelty*, Deleuze states that in "coining the term masochism, Krafft-Ebing was giving Sacher-Masoch credit for having redefined a clinical entity not merely in terms of the link between pleasure and pain, but in terms of something more fundamental," (16) yet his articulations of the perversion in *Psychopathia Sexualis* (1886) were ultimately too restrictive, reducing its etiology to the turning around of sadism's active/passive modality – what Deleuze later determined was a "clinical and semiological impossibility" (Studlar, 13). In 1924, Freud made a further attempt

26

to explain the condition in his treatise, "The Economic Problem of Masochism," addressing what he described as the "incomprehensible" character of the pathology: its utter defiance of the *pleasure principle*'s "first aim... the avoidance of unpleasure and the obtaining of pleasure," which would leave the pleasure principle "paralysed... as though the watchman over our mental life were put out of action by a drug" (159).

Expanding on earlier thinking, Freud's essay delineates a typology of three inter-related forms of masochism: the *erotogenic* or *primary* – which stems from an inversion of the sadistic instinct wherein the subject is doubled as the object of his or her own destruction, turning inward rather than outward, and finding "pleasure in pain" (161); the *feminine* – in which the subject "wants to be treated like a naughty child... also seeking pleasure in pain," but here through the performance of fantasies that can be "an end in themselves or serve to induce potency and lead to the sexual act"[31] (162); and the *moral* – which unlike the first two, need not "emanate from the [requests of the] loved person... [since] the suffering itself is what matters" (165). In this third modality, a latent tension between what Freud supposed was the essentially masochistic nature of the ego, and the sadism of the superego, manifests itself in the individual's sense of (unconscious) guilt. But while this elaborate demarcation may prove useful in naming or diagnosis, it returns us to the principal conundrum as each of the three variations remains rooted in the *primary* and its "counterpart in instinctual life" (163). And although not all psychoanalytic interpretations "link the process of turning around with the superego" they perpetuate Freud's theories "insofar as they retain the general hypothesis of a reversal of sadism" (Deleuze, 1971: 123).

With these thoughts in mind we return to Bess. Having been granted the right to marry Jan, she waits impatiently on the blustery tarmac in her wedding gown and veil. Set in a coastal village in the Outer Hebrides, a small group of islands off the north-west tip of the Scottish mainland, the film chronicles the coming-of-age of a sheltered innocent, inexperienced in matters sexual and romantic, who is swept into a passionate love affair with a man who in his supreme physicality is the precise embodiment of that from which her family has been trying to protect her. Temporally situated in the early 1970s – though in the scarcity of mod-cons and pop-cultural detritus, it feels peculiar and displaced – the location plays a symbolic role, always present and always judging, functioning as the locus of an unvarying tension; its grim austerity a reminder of the line not to be crossed, its geographical isolation emblematic of the passage not to be taken.

In his introduction to the published transcription of *Breaking the Waves*, von Trier declares that the film is "about good," (20) but the abstruseness of such a statement lies in how one understands this term when there is a wealth of connotations and denotations that can be assigned. For many women, "submission and purity are culturally encoded as prescriptive femininity... [some] become aware that they can never be *good* enough... [which can lead to] self-destructive behaviours" (Makarushka, from E. Ann Kaplan, 3). For Bess, the notion of *being* good is prescribed by the church, and synonymous with a religious altruism that demands the subordination of one's own needs without immunity. But in her intense love for Jan, and its manifestation in the sexual act, Bess encounters a new sensation, that of *feeling* good, and this discovery appears as miraculous and divine, for it arrives with a certainty that to this point has been reserved for the word of God.

Such newly-wedded bliss is not to last, however, as Jan is called back to the rigs, leaving Bess devastated and alone. Emotionally incapable of surviving without him, she prays for an intervention. In the solitude of the church pew, God speaks through her, "for many years you have prayed for love... you must learn to endure." But endurance is not an option now that Bess has been awakened to the pleasures of physical intimacy, and so she perseveres, "nothing else matters. I just want Jan home again." In uttering these fated words, she not only alters the direction of the narrative, but provides us with our first example of the affection-sound; which again is accompanied by the image of her face in close-up. For in speaking to God – this acousmêtre who may or may not exist but whose voice is channelled through Bess in whispered strokes – she communicates her secret desires as though directly into the viewer's ear. In doing so, the sound-image is read as affective because in its unmediated iconicity it empties the space that surrounds it and produces a momentary aural *any-space-whatever* whose parts are not fixed to any causality (Deleuze, 1986: 217). This is significant because, as was stated earlier, it is in these instances that the destabilizing properties of the time-image are perpetuated *within* the organic regime, thereby making us vulnerable to a deeper empathic response when we are forcefully thrust back into the narrative. Unfortunately for Bess, however, in perpetrating an act of such unpardonable selfishness, *God* is seen to have no other recourse than to punish the transgression. He sends Jan home – impotent, depressed, and paralyzed below the waist – with a caveat for Bess, "I had to test you. Your love for Jan has been put to the test."

And so Bess is made to suffer. But how can we articulate the terms of her misery? Investigating von Trier for sadistic intent is a possible avenue, but one that is ultimately unproductive, concentrating as it does on *his* psychological make-up and ignoring the meaning-making structures of the cinematic text. We could evaluate the connection between Bess and her "sadistic, misogynist deity" (Makarushka, 2) from a Freudian perspective, observing the embodiment of a *primary* sado-masochism in her two-voiced conversations; for as Bess makes audible both her own thoughts and those of God's, she becomes both the subject and the object of the destructive instinct. But having questioned the utility of this schema earlier, there seems little to be gained from additional elaboration. Leaving Freud's *feminine* and *moral* forms of masochism aside for now, we turn instead to the literature, seeking new insights into the *fundamental something* identified by Deleuze that differentiates the masochistic and sadistic texts.

Admirers of *pornographic* fiction, "a literature reduced to a few imperatives... followed by obscene descriptions" (Deleuze, 1971: 17) are mistaken when applying this term to the work of Sade and Sacher-Masoch. Deleuze posits the "more exalted title of *pornology* because its erotic language cannot be reduced to the elemental functions of ordering and describing" (18) and focuses the first half of his project on articulating the divergence of the two authors within this categorization. A definition of masochistic literature, as originated in the novels of Sacher-Masoch, is informed in large part by that which it is not: sadistic. With its almost mathematical illustration of the *idea* – in this instance, the "pure reason" of violence and its expression (which in truth can never be realized) – the linguistic objective of the Sadeian libertine is far removed from that of the masochistic hero, whose search for the *ideal* is made manifest by language, as in the negotiations of a "contracted alliance" between master and slave (21).[32] Consequently, the superlative state of existence sought by the masochist, in and through his relationships, seeks its primary execution in the realm of fantasy where it is freed from the disappointments of sadistic literature and its inevitable impotence.

Here, the sadistic text is understood as containing an explicit narrative pattern in which the previously outlined structure of pornographic literature is transcended through the insertion of passages written in a rigorously *demonstrative* language. Drawing on the terms prescribed by Deleuze in his summary of the two literary prototypes (134)[33] and the characteristics which differentiate them, we understand that with Sade, "the *negative* is all-pervasive, but the process of death and destruction is only a partial process... [and so] the perfect crime is impossible" (27). Hence the quest for this unattainable *pure negation* fuels the libertine's delusions and increases the body count as the *quantitative reiteration* of demonstration and its requisite actions leads to the repeated "destruction of nameless victims," (Studlar, 19) or in the case of *Justine*, the multiple rapes and beatings of the heroine amidst the brutalization of countless, faceless others. That there is ritual present in the murder and torture of the Sadeian woman is not in dispute, but this should not be confused with the fetishism that characterizes the masochistic text, which in its "process of disavowal and suspension of disbelief," displaces the fetishistic object rather than eradicating it (33). This need to persecute and destroy finds its psychoanalytic roots in the sadist's superego which, lacking the "moral character [of its] internal and complementary ego," repeatedly asserts itself, exercising its "cruelty to the fullest extent" (124). As Deleuze suggests, "the fundamental significance of sadistic apathy [is that] the sadist has no other ego than that of his victims [and] is thus monstrously reduced to pure superego which... recovers its full sexuality as soon as it diverts its power outward" (124).

Commendable for its "unusual decency," the masochistic text, though sometimes obscene in its description, is not automatically so, and with the exception of a "certain atmosphere of suffocation and suspense... [communicates its] "fantasies as though they were instances of national custom and folklore, or the innocent games of children," (25) standing in sharp contrast to the sadistic text and its institutionalized prescriptions. Here, Deleuze distinguishes a form of expression that is linguistically *qualitative*, seeking to suspend pleasure through a disavowal which prolongs the narrative foreplay (and delays its anticipated culmination) through the fetishizing of description, using language as both *persuasion* – in the teasing and enticement of the torturer into the masochistic contract which "represents the ideal form of the love-relationship and its necessary precondition" – and *imagination*, in the telling of a fantasy "for its own sake," (75) or the elaboration of dreams. In Sacher-Masoch's *Venus in Furs*, Severin compares his torment to that of Samson, evoking the familiarity of history and myth, "of art... the immobile and reflective quality of culture (70).[34] With the citing of such lineage, Severin locates himself within a tradition of cultivated and moral men for whom the state of want, and the anxiety its realization creates, becomes the object of pleasure – the "ego triumphs and the superego [with its attendant cruelty] can only appear from outside" (125).

The problem now, having summarized the distinctions between these two literary precedents, is how to engage this knowledge – the solution is best proffered in the form of a riddle: if we are to accept Deleuze's hypothesis that the conventional understanding of the sado-masochistic construct cannot possibly exist, that the two are in fact mutually exclusive, can we demarcate a unique discursive space for the co-existence of these two clearly independent textual bodies – one sadistic, the other masochistic – within one bipartite filmic structure, and thus a conception of *Breaking the Waves* that locates its expression in this thematic collision? And provided this supposition does hold up under scrutiny, can we also surmise that this *intertextual* dialogue is the motor by which our spectatorial response is engendered? The answer is yes. In repeatedly traversing this intertextual border, the cinematic text generates the expressive rupture obligatory to this newly-articulated post-modern paradigm. In doing so, it entraps the viewer in a state of perpetual displacement and disorientation: *between* the sadistic text with its "momentum of repetition [that] tends to force us onto the side of the torturer," and the masochistic, in which "the art of suspense always places us on the side of the victim" (Deleuze, 1971: 34). But where do we go from here? How can we situate this new sado-masochistic entity so that it intersects with the two planes of the binary-chain?

Perhaps the easiest way to begin is by elucidating the correspondence between the two on the most basic level – that is to say, for reasons soon to be made clear, the sadistic text locates its allegiance with the relational objects along the empathic plane, while the masochistic text aligns itself with those that make up the affective. Essentially, what we have on the one hand is a textual body that seeks to debase and destroy. This is the heterocosm of the movement-image, of the sadistic narrative. It expresses itself through repeated and ritualistic acts of cruelty – brutalizing Bess (and later, Selma) as it seeks its ultimate goal: pure negation. But we must take this one step further, for this is a project whose focus is sound. Hence, we can argue that the sadistic text finds its aural manifestation primarily in the arena of diegetic sound; for in the formation and maintenance of an organic causality, the mise-en-bande assists the narrative in the work of ordering, and the continuity of events. It does not need to "prove anything to anyone, but [only] to perform a demonstration related essentially to the solitude and omnipotence of its author" (Deleuze, 1971: 19). Concurrently, the crystalline regime seeks to describe and displace, to fetishize rather than obliterate. This is the realm of the time-image, of the *masochistic aesthetic* – a dominion that is "persuasive, aesthetically-oriented, and centred around the idealizing, mystical exaltation" of that which cannot be otherwise expressed (Studlar, 18).[35] And so the affective plane can be posited as that which embodies this masochistic aesthetic, because in its use of more poetic visuals and lyrical aural forms, it expresses itself as an act of fantasy and imagination.

But what if we disagree with the rigidity of Deleuze's conclusions with regard to the *impossibility* of the sado-masochistic construct? There is certainly a precedent to do so. The labour of recognition and naming is confused by a suspicion that characteristics of Sade and Sacher-Masoch are present on both textual planes. This raises a line of enquiry that is germane to both films: if this new paradigmatic entity can be described as containing both sadistic and masochistic elements, we are freed from the constraints of a too narrow methodology and able to analyse the films using a model based on the substantially more elastic prototype articulated in the last chapter. Such speculations in no way detract from the efforts made so far, nor do they discredit the scholarship of Deleuze who has argued against this dichotomy in other contexts, and whose *Masochism*, it must be acknowledged, focuses exclusively on the primary canonical texts, rather than the appropriations and metamorphoses of their various heirs. Thus, this sado-masochistic entity can be read as complementary rather than oppositional and take its place along the binary-chain.

empathic plane	sadism	spoken language
↕	↕	↕
affective plane	masochism	musical language

This new-found autonomy also helps facilitate understandings of how the textual components interact within this new explicitly sado-masochistic (or maso-sadistic) framework, and allows for the occurrence of heretofore *impossible* notions: such as the identification of a Sadeian heroine[36] within an otherwise masochistic text, or the categorization of the narrative sequences as sadistic despite our awareness that the central couples – Bess and Jan, and Selma and Bill – are engaged in relationships that we might describe as mutually masochistic, "regulated by contracts that formalize and verbalize the behaviour of the partners" (Deleuze, 1971: 18). And so we have created a modality for investigating the nature of these pairings, but before doing so, must further elucidate the thematic resonances of the film's mise-en-bande.

When we last saw Bess, she was crouched on the church floor thanking God for saving Jan's life. Despite the punishing words he had just (though not justly) inflicted on her, she wears a smile of serene confidence, indicative of both a knowing contentment, and of the movement-image's shift from affection to action. Then, with an abrupt edit – for dissolves and fades to black would be too harmonious – our return to the narrative is halted. In this moment, we are disengaged from its empathic grasp and resituated in another magnificent landscape so arresting in its stillness that it is only after several seconds of staring at the dark purple sky that the appearance of a rainbow, temporarily displaced by passing clouds, reminds us that we are indeed watching a moving picture. As is the case with each of the time-images, this one is partnered with a short piece of non-diegetic seventies-era glam rock – "A Whiter Shade of Pale" by Procul Harem – that is somehow reassuring in its familiarity, and yet seems strange and out of place in the context of this diegesis. Here, the fetishizing nature of the time-sound replaces the ordering voices of the narrative with a fantasy-like interlude that sends our undirected thoughts spiralling and fragmenting into the space-time. However, there is something more going on here as well, for this is not just a few bars of orchestral music, but rather a well-known pop song – a small chunk of music history that reverberates not only in the meaning-making structures of the instrumentation and the melody, but through a whole host of intertextualities and resonances that are contained in both the lyrical content, and in the echoes of the singer's voice. The question now is to whom do we turn for insight on how to articulate these manifold layers of resonance?

Film music studies, to use its pedagogical referent, has been hiding in the shadow of film studies for decades, in part because of cinema's legacy as a visual medium whose first thirty years were silent, but also due to the fact that for the most part, film scholars have never fully come to terms with the role that sound plays in the cinema, other than to have it absorbed into our collective subconscious to the point of its disappearance from the critical horizon. Yet, although the study of film sound is relatively new, a small number of theorists have been writing about it since the early thirties when ideas regarding the practice of composing and placing film music were first formalized and documented as a classical methodology – not to mention earlier texts that instructed musicians on when to include which types of music as accompaniment for silent films. That being said, on the whole, the study of the mise-en-bande has been marginalized by film scholars unfamiliar with the vocabulary, and/or musicologists still stubbornly attached to the notion of *absolute* music, which unencumbered by any sort of dramatic or visual representation, solidifies their "resistance to musical *meaning*" (Buhler, 2003: 73). Michel Chion, whose work has actively sought out and built a new vocabulary for sound studies is a notable exception, as are the film-sound theoreticians who have followed in his footsteps (Claudia Gorbman and Rick Altman, to name just a few). Yet in most of the scholarship to date there has still been little attention paid to the use of popular – or more specifically, *sung* songs – at least in the academic milieu. Even Gorbman, whose work deals exclusively with the relationship between music and the filmic text only marginally attends to the subject, stating that these "songs require narrative to cede to spectacle… and therefore threaten to offset the aesthetic balance between music and narrative cinematic representation" (20). But this is clearly not the case in *Breaking the Waves*. In fact, because the diegetic sequences still strictly adhere to the Dogme prescription, there is no *theme* music whatsoever in the organic regime; it is only the chapter headings that are of import to this discussion, and so it is necessary to look elsewhere for a workable approach.

I originally turned to the work of John Izod, whose Jungian-psychoanalytic analysis of the *image-chains* in the films of Nicolas Roeg provides a useful schema for enunciating the complex workings of the cinematic text that is easily appropriated here. He uncovers significance in the linking of visual tropes to their thematic referents: such as the "red-blood-warmth-fire-life" and "red-blood-danger-stop-death" chains he classifies in Roeg's *Don't Look Now*, suggesting that meaning can also be unearthed in the *audio-chains* which develop out of the mise-en-bande. What became evident, however, as my reading of Izod progressed, was that the Deleuzian model and the psychoanalytic are in many ways incompatible.[37] This issue also raised its head when working through Gaylyn Studlar's *In The Realm of Pleasure*, which also draws heavily on psychoanalytic theory "to expand and enrich Deleuze's theory" (Studlar, 9). That said, these two works have nonetheless been instrumental to this thesis as their respective lexicons directly influenced the creation of new concepts which have in turn played a significant role in the development of my methodological approach. In fact, I have already employed a version of Izod's construct in my conception of the binary-chain, but in a schematic sense, what the audio-chain offers is an opportunity to move vertically away from the horizon of the binary-chain, allowing for greater ease in extracting and mapping coherences of theme and structure.

For example, in the first of many possible audio-chains, the non-diegetic music which characterizes the sound-images of the crystalline regime (and the diegetic music of the organic plane) connects us first to the character of Bess, and then to the freedom she seeks to inherit in the modern world. More than a century ago, as European society was approaching a new millennium and the metropolis as we know it was starting to take shape, women were virtually absent from the urban landscape, confined to their kitchens and parlours, and "forced to forego the lure of aimless strolling without a specific purpose or destination" (Gleber, 62) – the pleasurable domain of the *flâneur*. What experience of city life these women were able to enjoy was mediated by the desires and conditions of their male companions – for it was only prostitutes who walked the darkened streets alone – who offered an ingress into this modern world, but also set the price. Though the two films examined here are made to feel contemporary through their use of post-modern techniques and displaced localizations of time and space, they are essentially period pieces: with *Breaking the Waves* set in the seventies, and *Dancer in the Dark* in the sixties. What also unites these films is that to some extent they can be read as cautionary tales about societies who are teetering on the cusp of modernity yet somewhat resistant to its advances – morally, technologically and judicially. Bess and Selma can be read as the very embodiment of this moment, and they are punished in part for their forward-thinking as they seek entrance into this new world: on their own terms, and with their integrity intact.

In *Breaking the Waves*, language becomes the arena wherein the oppression of women is undertaken, and Jan, the conduit through which Bess – a *flâneuse* seeking to "indulge her full fascination" (Gleber, 62) – locates her point of entry. In the beginning, Jan enthusiastically embraces his role: taking Bess to the movies, buying her a fashionable dress, and offering her his music. Soon, however, the verbal expression of his desires and conditions becomes as restrictive as those of his forefathers[38] – for the "street does not *belong* to women" and neither does the right to speech: "they cannot take possession of it freely without also expecting to be impeded by public judgements" (Gleber, 61). And so like a sexual assault victim who is re-victimized by her rapists' lawyer because she walked home from work one night, Bess is seen to have "asked for it" – not in bringing about the monstrous beating which leads to her death, but in the singular act of choosing Jan, a husband from the "outside" who could facilitate her journey into modernity. Eventually, as I will discuss in more detail later in the chapter, the time-sound releases her from this sentence and delivers "Bess the virgin" to the kingdom of heaven – for like Justine, "when against her will she is fucked, she knows she remains good because she does not feel pleasure" (Carter, 48).[39]

In a second audio-chain, the patriarchal tradition that employs words to dominate and brand, is tracked through the vococentric nature of the organic regime's sadistically reiterative discourse,[40] finding its ultimate manifestation in Bess's perceived transgressions and their articulation in the language which drives "Bess the whore" from the house of God, and sentences her to the eternal damnations of hell. Here, the relational character of the binary-chain permits us to transcend the Cartesian split that perpetuates the dichotomy of body and mind, for in Bess, they are inexorably and eternally intertwined. Instead, she is read as a body-without-organs (or BwO), neither concept nor state, but "a practice, a set of practices" (Deleuze and Guattari, 1987: 150). Consequently, Bess – and Jan, for he too becomes a BwO – operate in this newly articulated sadistic space as *masochistic* bodies: bodies of desire, of fetishization, and becoming (154).

The BwO is identified here as a masochistic body precisely because it is a becoming body that both seeks desire, and at the same time, is desire (1987: 165). Yet there are contradictions between the thinking in "How do you Make Yourself a Body-Without-Organs?" from *A Thousand Plateaus* (Deleuze and Guattari, 1987) and the much earlier *Masochism* (Deleuze, 1971).[41] In the later text, Deleuze and Guattari seem reconciled to that *impossible* sado-masochistic entity that Deleuze refutes in the earlier work, stating that the BwO which is identified as a "masochistic body... has its sadist or whore sew it up" (150). Later in the chapter, the BwO is described as desiring both "its own annihilation" and "the power to annihilate" (165) – desires that are traditionally attributed to the masochist and the sadist, respectively, and seem to bring us back to those problems raised by Freud's primary inversion. What this ultimately suggests is that it is increasingly arduous to fully resolve these manifold tensions. In the end, however, what is most valuable, is to acknowledge that some ambiguity is likely to remain despite our best efforts. And so we proceed with the good will and optimism necessary to traverse such difficult philosophical terrain, and return to the sadistic text.

Deleuze says that "words are at their most powerful when they compel the body to repeat the movements they suggest" (1971: 18). When Jan recovers his libido, but due to the paralysis is incapable of satisfying his sexual urges, words are all he has to wield. In his first entreaty, he implores Bess to take a lover, "find a man to make love to, then come back here and tell me about it. It will be like you and me being together." But for Bess, spoken language is equated with pain and oppression – in the strictures of the church, and the diagnoses of doctors who seek to shield her from "feeling too much." In her world, the patriarchy is ubiquitious and supreme, intent on keeping her forever "stupid" and mute – whereas her love for Jan offers a truer sense of freedom and security in its promise of pleasure and escape. So when Jan mimics this male establishment in his use of such explicit terminology, it is felt as a betrayal; for Bess's "exploration of the world ends where it encounters its limitations in [men]... whose fantasies assault, annoy, disturb, and perpetually evaluate her" (Gleber, 74). Yet what motivates Jan is not the sadist's requisite need for cruelty, but rather the "suspense factor" of masochism in which the anxiety of waiting and delay creates sexual tension and inhibits its discharge (Deleuze, 1971: 75).[42] This was effective when Jan was separated from Bess before the accident, but has become imperative now that any discharge of sexual tension has been made physically impossible by the accident. And though his prescriptive language to Bess can be read as sadistic in character, it is too simplistic to read her position as that of the passive victim.

That chunks of diegetic music[43] are sometimes inserted into these sadistic sequences does provide us (and Bess) with some reprieve from the punishing trajectory of the narrative, though it is never derailed from its punitive course. Yet, because these moments can be read again as an intercession by the time-image, we recognize them as ultimately destabilizing elements that make us once more vulnerable to the narrative events still to come. Early in the film, while snuggled in bed and fantasizing of Jan's return, Bess clutches the radio close to her ear, fashioning a private sanctuary in which she can commune with him, as though she were certain that somewhere in the night he was listening to the same song. But this moment is short-lived, sandwiched as it is by out-of-sequence shots of Bess in the town's phone booth waiting anxiously for his call, and then afterward, whispering awkward sexual nothings into the receiver, trying out this new lingua franca, rolling the words around her tongue with the delight of a small child sucking on a hard candy.

In this instance, words take on the colour of music as Bess and Jan communicate through a symbolic exchange of forbidden sounds, and the intimacies of shared breath; and as it with music, the pleasures are deeply felt. For here is the location of our second type of affection-sound. Taking place within the primary text – as opposed to that which engages in transtextual dialogue – the voice in close-up is nonetheless affective because of its intrinsic firstness which "refers to itself," and in doing so, becomes a sound-image that is understood as one of "pure possibility" (Deleuze, 1989: 30). Yet in terms of the audience's response, there is something else going on as well, for these illicit sounds can also be read – an activity of cognitive thought – as participating in the audio-chain that equates musical forms of expression with freedom, sexuality, and the prospect of better days to come. What this means is that we now have two demonstrations of a possible engagement: one felt and one thought. Hence, in the organic regime which contains these affection-sounds, we can understand our spectatorial response in the context of Worringer's *positive* empathy because the musicality of the language enables an experience of self-activated pleasure (6). And so what appears at first to be an irreconcilable contradiction is instead an indication of one of the affective body's essential truths: that despite the controlling structures of the movement-image, the sensing body can never be completely overridden by the conscious body.

Later, Bess will ease into her first (and last) attempt at seduction with a slug of whiskey and Elton John on the turntable. Whirling around Dr. Richardson's living room, she is suddenly rapturous, the soul taken over by the body which gains the audacity to undress. But with the hurried silencing of the record, her already transitory courage is cut short. Rebuked by Dr. Richardson, she returns to Jan with nothing erotic to report. Were Bess to have been given the opportunity to express herself musically – like Selma in *Dancer in the Dark* – this would be a probable moment for her to escape into song; allowing the rhythms of the melody to nourish her imagination. In doing so, as the time-sounds of the affective regime constructed the masochistic fantasy, they would be able to penetrate the chain of movement-images and send their slender fingers down to ease Jan's need. As it is, Bess tries to fabricate some tantalizing descriptions, but is betrayed by the limits of her idiolect, for she has only just entered this world of language, and "requires an additional measure of physical and psychological confidence: the initial courage to step out, to face the threat of assault, or erase her latent misrecognition as a prostitute" (Gleber, 60). Jan has taught her the only sexual phrases that she knows, and when she repeats them back to him, unable to engage the musicality that characterized their verbal lovemaking prior to the accident, he sees through her tepid ruse.

There is no music at all when Bess makes her successful foray into adultery, just that unforgiving wind, the dull rumble of an old bus engine, and the relentless squeak of seats as the wheels bumpety-bump over the rough-hewn road. Devoted to the work of keeping Jan alive, Bess seeks only the wordless completion of her task, forcing her hand into the crotch of a mutely accepting stranger. Here we experience what Worringer calls *negative* empathy because our desire to *alienate* ourselves from the unpleasantness of the narrative is overwhelmed; broken by the force of its demands, we are abandoned to that which we cannot control - *unpleasure* (6). Shortly after, Bess returns to the hospital where she recounts the details of her recent transgression using Jan's name instead of the old man's, thereby making him the imagined recipient of this now solicited offering, and enabling her to employ the provocative language in a convincing and meaningful manner. There are many possible explanations as to why Bess eventually acquiesces to Jan's desires but they are speculative at best. Instead, we look outside of the film for answers, to Angela Carter, whose interrogations of Sade's novels provide a new paradigm from which to approach our discussion of Bess.

It is again important to note that Carter's monograph, *Sadeian Women and the Ideology of Pornography*, also finds an awkward fit when positioned alongside the work of Deleuze (and Guattari) yet despite these tensions and possible incompatibilities, her reading of the sadistic heroine is extremely useful and easily appropriated here. Unlike Deleuze, Carter does not concern herself with the polemic surrounding the sado-masochistic entity, describing Justine's suffering as a "kind of mastery" that can be seen as a "masochistic mastery over herself" (50). Seeking to understand and perhaps empower the heroines of sadistic fiction through her research, her essay interrogates the inherent paradoxes in Sade's construction of femininity. For Carter, "Justine is a good woman in a man's world. She is a good woman according to the rules laid down by men and her reward is rape, humiliation, and incessant beatings" (38). In many ways, she could be talking about Bess, who "always does what she is told... because that is the nature of her own definition of goodness" (55). But how far can this comparison take us?

Earlier, the notion of a *mutual* masochism was raised as a possible enunciation of the central pairings in the two films, but it is the relationship between Bess and Jan that is most easily addressed using this model. Based on observation rather than previously articulated scholarship, this concept was introduced as a means for attending to the complexities of these relationships and how they might provide insight into the two heroines. It is easy to think of

Bess as a *masochist* in the popular construction of the term because there is an agency to her actions that seems to point toward this verdict, but when you look for analogous characters in *Venus in Furs* – which is seen as the ur-text of masochistic literature – the process of naming is revealed to be much more complex. On the surface, Bess does not appear to have anything in common with Severin, the hero of *Venus in Furs*, yet in her love for Jan, and her experience of a very real pain that is inextricably entwined with the pleasures of keeping Jan alive, the paradox of the masochistic construct is made concrete. That their relationship can also be turned around is what led to speculation of a masochistic mutuality, for it is equally viable to talk about the Bess/Jan pairing in light of Severin's relationship with Wanda: Jan uses persuasive language to convince Bess to enter into their post-accident contract and then faces, or at least seeks, a sort of pleasure/pain amalgam in having her talk explicitly about her sexual adventures with other men. But again, Bess finds an equally awkward fit with the despotic Wanda who is "sensual yet cool" and partakes in no *suffering* until she runs away to Paris in search of her own submission (Studlar, 22). And so we return to Justine "who always hopes her good behaviour will procure her some reward, some respite from the bleak and intransigent reality which surrounds her," (55) but is not spared, surviving years of torture and debasement only to be struck down by lightening in the supposed safety of her sister's home.

And yet Justine retains an (albeit misguided) faith in the supremacy of her own goodness; a virtue maintained by simply "doing what she is told" (Carter, 47). The same can be said of Bess, and so we can recognize a variation of the Sadeian heroine who discovers that the "world was not... made for [her] and who do[es] not have, because [she] has not been given, the existential tools to remake the world for [herself]" (Carter, 57) – despite her intense longing to do so. But if we are content to align Bess with this quintessential image of female victimization, must we then automatically consign Jan the function of the sadistic master? Not necessarily. From the moment of their first onscreen meeting, Jan's contribution to Bess's education has been through the introduction of a language distasteful to the zealous piety of the community: musical, sexual and profane. And so Jan begins his (diegetic) life as a conduit to the modern world, a role that sees him condemned in the eyes of Bess's friends and family. Later, his paralysis renders him more sympathetic, and it is in this moment that he assumes his place at the centre of his own masochistic fantasies, needing to believe that "he is dreaming even when he is not" (Deleuze, 1971: 72).[44] That Jan employs descriptive

40

and persuasive speech in his *manipulation* of Bess leads to his identification as a masochistic hero within this otherwise sadistic text. And so he is read as both victim and victimizer; the unwitting voice of the organic regime's ordered trajectory, who like the dubious hero of Kubrick's *A Clockwork Orange*, is held captive by the narrative and forced to witness the persecution that he alone has made possible, forced to exist within "the very depths of guilt" (Deleuze, 1971: 101) as at the same time, he gains gratification (and salvation) from Bess's sexual and corporeal sacrifice.

In the end, however, despite our propensity for romanticizing Bess as a victim, she remains somehow in control of her destiny – engaging in these risky behaviours regardless of how detrimental they may be to her physical and emotional health. Even as she is banished from church and home, she nourishes herself with a faith in her ability to endure that is sacrosanct, and seems to embrace the position that "at least the girl who sells herself with her eyes wide open is not a hypocrite" (Carter, 58). Her sister-in-law and Dr. Richardson try to intervene, but Bess has stopped listening to their entreaties, explaining that "God gives everyone a talent." When Dr. Richardson, who has lost the ability to speak tenderly to Bess, asks if her *talent* includes "being screwed by men [she has] never seen before," her response puts the discussion to rest: my talent, is that "I can believe." And so we can think her form of masochism as a variation on Freud's third designation: the *moral*. For here it is not the suffering that is "enough," but rather the capacity for suffering that sustains. But what of the audience; what sustains us as viewers? *Breaking the Waves* – especially in its decisive concluding scenes – is an extremely difficult and upsetting film to watch, but can we demarcate this experience as one of suffering? What is important now before moving onto *Dancer in the Dark* is to examine how the sado-masochistic construction of *Breaking the Waves* influences the spectatorial event in ways that are both unique to this film and shared by both.

The narrative is exceedingly cruel in the third act, following through with its brutal and punitive course despite the tenacity of Bess's faith. This is where the sadistic text finds its most explicit manifestation in *Breaking the Waves*. With no music, diegetic or otherwise, to provide solace, her body (though not her resolve) is weakened through a succession of increasingly violent and debased sexual encounters. In fact, there is no respite at all in this closing section, not even the voice of God, who has temporarily abandoned this "little thing called Bess" whose neediness has made it impossible for him to complete his other work. As she is ferried to the site of her final brutalization, she carries with her a keen awareness of what this journey will ultimately mean for her, and a barely lucid *knowledge* of what it portends for Jan – for Bess's final transformation into the BwO has already begun. She is no longer a consciously thinking creature, only a watching body whose movements are compelled by an energy she no longer has any control over. In these irrevocable moments, she speaks once more to God, seeking only companionship: "But you're with me now… Of course I am, Bess. You know that."

By this point in the narrative, Bess has fully engaged with the modern world – her entry marked not only by the transgressions of her body, but through the expression of that body in the form of spoken language. She stands up to her friends and family in those final moments before her return to the barge, and to the church elders as well, demanding to be told why they choose to "love a word" when the only thing that one can really love "is another human being." But this does not mean that she escapes punishment. Staggering toward her death with tear-stained eyes, torn fishnet stockings, and broken heels – accoutrement of the trade, borrowed from the town's only prostitute – she too pays the price of desire, the price of modernity. Later, in the moments before her death, Bess discovers that Jan is still dying despite her sacrifice, and resigned to that which she was never able to concede before, she speaks these immutable, tragic words: "I was wrong." And so we say our goodbyes to Bess, shattered by the realization that our sacrifice has also been in vain – having sat through this punishing and vindictive film, only to have our hopes extinguished as the last vestiges of breath pass her battered lips. Yet, all is not lost, for Bess's "poor show as a prostitute… is proof in itself that her heart is made of gold" and so we believe that she must somehow be made to endure (Carter, 66). Armed with this knowledge, and the perseverance of the masochistic text, our hope is restored by the realization that there is something more to come: an intercession by the crystalline regime to overturn the wicked assumptions of the organic.

There are a total of eight time-images that intersect this narrative, dividing the film into nine distinct sections. The final of these chapter headings is straightforward in its symbolism and quietly optimistic in tone: the image of a small creek flowing under an old stone bridge on a sunny spring morning, accompanied by Elton John's "Your Song" on the mise-en-bande. At this juncture, the watching non-conscious body feels absolutely no compulsion to narrativize the onscreen action, having come to terms with the masochistic

42

regime's intrusions and its function in the bipartite text – relieved to be offered an escape from the organic regime's merciless conclusions, and sucked into the at least momentarily calming swirls of the eddy. For this sensing body must always be understood as a "body in movement – there is only movement and rest, not stoppage" (Manning). What resonates here is how the signifying structures of the time-sound are felt by the viewer, especially in the case of songs which again are so recognizable that they hold us in their layers of evocative nameless intertextualities; embraced by that which is outside of the narrative – Elton John's voice, the rich tones of the piano, the echoes of history and geography; expressions of love and being loved – and sustained in this instance by incommensurable thought. In many ways, these vertically-resonant "intertextualities" connect us to the audio-chains discussed earlier, but these, however useful, are instruments for a cognitive analysis of the thematic linkages found primarily in the movement-images of the organic regime. What we seek instead is something to articulate the more sensorial experience engendered by these sounds – the way they make us feel, rather than the way they make us think.

Turning to Deleuze, we can redress these time-images as recollection-images, because they "refer us back to a former present" that has a "deeper" memory than what is enabled, for example, by the "feeble" flashback (Deleuze, 1989: 39). They are intertextual, if we allow that all aspects of art and life, whether lived or dreamed, can be read as text. This conception may not completely align itself with the specific nature of Deleuze's concept, since he does not recognize intertextuality, at least not explicitly – yet it is tremendously valuable in this modality. In "Transgressing Goodness," Irena Makarushka described the chapter headings as "postcard images that… remind viewers that the story is an old one" (8). She is not altogether wrong – though her conclusions are less relevant than that which she locates in the postcard and its attempt to capture a moment past. For in each of the time-images, "there corresponds a virtual memory-image (mental and subjective) recollected from chains of associations and memories of past experiences" (Rodowick, 90). The recollection-sound, when located in music, is the time-sound *par excellence* because in its many evolutions we experience the ephemera of history as vast and incalculable as the cosmos; the "greatness and brevity and eternal passing of everything [that is] vitally felt" (Dyer, quoting Suzanne K. Langer, 178).[45]

The recollection-image and its incongruities, such as the fact that it speaks of subjectivities while the time-image is understood as that which allows only for collective affect, will be discussed in greater detail in the following chapter. For now it is sufficient to state that the recollection-image, while still functioning as a time-image, can also be a source of great comfort, not just because it offers amnesty from the *unpleasures* of the narrative, but for the reason that it allows the mind to wander through this vast space-time of past experience as though floating through an exquisite dreamscape. Yet earlier, when discussing the role of the time-image in the spectatorial experience, I described it as that which creates a vulnerability to the sadism inherent in the movement-image, and so locates our suffering in the instability that its interval produces. The question now is how to resolve this resolutely esoteric contradiction? The problem lies in trying to tie this discussion down to something so tangible, for it must be acknowledged that the idea of suffering that we are trying to articulate here is perhaps too abstract for such a tidy précis. Yet attempting to do so is the very goal of this project, and so we must persist.

In essence, we suffer precisely because we are *always-already* becoming bodies and so we experience empathy when engaged with the movement-image, and at the same time, are released into ourselves by the crystalline. These shifts – no matter how reassuring in the moment, no matter which of the diverse images has characterized our engagement – are nevertheless destabilizing on the whole, striking at the very foundation of conscious thought and leaving us outside, more vulnerable along the surface of our skin. And in this confusion, in the any-space-whatever between the sadistic and the masochistic – we suffer. For we too are held prisoner: both victimizer and victimized, conflicted on a level beyond language, experiencing a guilt which cannot be expressed and a complicity that cannot be defended or denied.

In the final chunk of narrative that follows the time-image described above, we are shocked to discover a fully-recovered Jan as he stands watch over Bess's reluctant burial at the hands of the church elders; who after much impassioned negotiation, agree to bury Bess, but refuse to go against the edicts of the church, consigning her soul to hell. Later, Jan and his friends dig up Bess's coffin and take her back with them to the rig, where they bless her soul and offer her body to the sea. That night, as the men sleep, they are awakened by a glorious ringing of bells across the water, a ghostly sound, disconnected from the diegesis but no longer distraught. For the viewer in these moments there is nothing to see on the horizon, just the vast reaches of the ocean, its waves churning as though in response to the violent requests of the dark purple sky. Here, we can think of Bess as having been displaced by the ringing bell, the fetishistic object, symbolic and eternal. As the bells continue to call out to the immeasurable landscape, Bess is returned to her rightful state as a BwO – a body caught in a "strange state of indeterminacy" (Deleuze, 1971: 26) – thereby disabling the total eradication sought by the narrative and finding the sadistic text once more left impotent. In doing so, we are tendered a narrative closure that allows the emotions generated by the film to be absorbed, while allowing Bess the BwO to be free to become eternal (and eternally become). But how does this complex process work?

There is something miraculous that occurs on the horizon of the mise-en-bande in this epilogue , something akin to what we witnessed in *Caché* – with its "deceptive" time-image – yet strikingly different. For here, what appears at first to be a movement-image and movement-sound, is transformed by the intrusion of a recollection-sound (an image of time) in the mise-en-bande. This is a fundamental point, and it must be clearly elucidated: the movement-image need not always correspond to a movement-sound. As will be argued in the chapter on *Dancer in the Dark*, it is this surprising collision between the time-sound and the organic regime that has allowed for the musical to express itself. In *Breaking the Waves*, as the otherworldly bells replace the diegetic movement-sounds, the final image is transformed from one of movement to one of time – releasing Bess from the grip of the narrative's sadistic conclusions, and in doing so, providing us with a sense of something that is difficult to describe, but that would otherwise be impossible to experience. Yet this is not a conscious thought, for in the affective moment, we experience this sensation as merely that, a sensation of the skin, of breath, and of the body. We may want to name it: to call it hope, or beauty, or understanding, but we cannot. It will always, must always, remain nameless. That said, this does not reduce or diminish its affective powers, and so it remains forever anonymous, yet profoundly meaningful nonetheless.

What is that noise? The wind under the door. What is that noise now?
What is the wind doing? Nothing again nothing. Do you know nothing?
Do you see nothing? Do you remember nothing?

- T. S. Eliot

CHAPTER THREE

Dancer in the Dark – Memory, Genre, and the Silencing of the Female Voice

As mentioned in chapter one, the cinematic sound-image can be recognized in a diversity of modes: in music, in spoken language, and in all the other possible types of recordable sound. It can also be located in silence. T.S. Eliot speaks to this complexity in *The Wasteland*, his modernist masterpiece from 1922. Here, silence is equated with the improbably quantifiable percept of nothingness. The key component of the word lies in its root, that which names it as a concept: thing. It is at the same time a no-thing whatsoever (absence) and yet a *nothing* (presence) – both intangible and yet concrete. On the mise-en-bande, this nothingness can be read as either the absence of sound, or the presence of what we might call *soundlessness*. This distinction becomes especially exigent in the case of filmic texts where the traditional understanding of silence is simply that which precludes voice and action. But this type of soundscape is in fact meticulously constructed using room tone – the sound which is recorded live on location while no one is speaking or moving (though physical and mechanical breath is captured)[46] – and other forms of so-called natural sound. It is not silence.

When one encounters true silence in a film, as we do at the end of *Dancer in the Dark*, we are submitted to an aural experience that is entirely new – though at the same time, as old as the cinema itself, harkening back to the era of the kinetoscope and the penny arcade, before the first noted instance of a musical accompaniment on December 28, 1885 (Brown,

12). Here, there is no sound whatsoever coming from the screen: no hum, no throb, no echo of lived events – there is only soundlessness, and of course, the utterances, spoken or otherwise, emitting from the audience. And it is this which makes the viewing of this film such a formidable spectatorial experience, because it is in these moments that we become hyper-aware of the collectivity of sensing bodies surrounding us; we may not see them with our eyes, but we are with them nonetheless. Fostering an increased understanding of the recollection-sound, and its intertextual faculties, as well as the insights elucidated by Michel Chion and others as to the function of silence in the cinema, this chapter sustains the sado-masochistic construction introduced earlier, but takes its analysis one step further. By investigating how the play of memory behaves in tandem with the generic tropes of the melodramatic and musical forms, we can better understand how the destabilized viewer's empathic engagement makes the shock of the ending so much more palpable and traumatic. And, as mentioned in the last chapter, in our recognition of a new degree of agency in Selma, we are offered further occasions for thinking about the nature of her character. But first, the film.

What is easy to forget by the end of *Dancer in the Dark* is that it begins in a truly remarkable fashion: with a collage of painterly images lasting three minutes and thirty-eight seconds, a fairly protracted duration considering this is essentially a narrative film with the expectations that such works generate in the audience. The initial sequence, whose images are layered one on top of the other rather than laid out in a horizontal chain – the very delineation of Deleuze's *duration* – functions almost as an inverted coda,[47] able to stand up on its own as a thing of both thematic resonance and aesthetic beauty: a short exercise in experimental cinema at its most majestic and affecting.

It begins with sound. The instrumental strains of the overture are heard first, followed shortly after by the emergence of a pure white screen: the empty canvas upon which the artist constructs his (and our collective) vision. The low hum of a single tuba sets the stage. Specks of black begin to appear as though coaxed out of hiding by the beseeching tones. Then the French horns join the refrain, and the image starts to take form – shapes in deliberate transformation that are always on the verge of meaning yet remain assiduously outside of logic or causality. For what we are witnessing in these first few moments is an exemplar of Deleuze's time-image "in its simplest manifestation: an autonomous shot describing a single event as simple duration" (Rodowick, 14). The audience watches, incredulous, not knowing

48

what to make of this foray into abstraction. Are these clues that will resonate more forcefully in later scenes? Is there an impending episode that will produce a framework for these images and their significance? For some viewers there may be no engagement at all in these early moments – the film as white noise providing only that which is seen as "necessary" at this stage: a backdrop to the business of settling in before the "real" work, that which is demanded by the narrative, commences. But regardless of how present the spectator is in these moments, the text has surreptitiously engaged us with its task. For even white noise has the capacity for effect; distracting the mind from its contextual space, and in doing so, separating cognizant thought from the senses, but not from sensorial experience – leaving that which can only occur in this instance, unconstrained and absolute: affect. But to truly understand this process, we must look more closely at the scene's dyadic construct.

We begin with the mise-en-bande. The overture is clearly a music of becoming as one instrument's departure makes way for another's arrival – the ebb and flow as a dialogue that continues without stoppage until it eventually fades into soundlessness, the quintessence of the sound-image's incommensurability. The same can be said of the mise-en-scène. Cinematically speaking, the dissolve is always in a process of becoming, distinct from the cut which is simply the replacement of one image with another. In a narrative sequence, the dissolve functions as an ellipsis, connecting movement-images in a still causal chain that moves the action forward more quickly than the cut. On this empathic plane, there are places of rest between these dissolves, moments when we are provided with an opportunity for focused and reflective thought, when we are able to fully take in the surroundings, assembling the fragments of narrativized information into recognizable and cogent patterns. In the time-image, however, there are no moments of stasis or even rest, and nothing whatsoever upon which to focus our thinking. It is a thoroughly affective and affecting space-time.

In these moments, the dissolve overlaps (and overlaps again) so that the object is always replaced, "continually *erasing* it, and creating it anew" (Rodowick, 90). Hence the image – which is merely strata suspended in the becoming present, "what is *before* and what is *after*" (Deleuze, 1989: 38) – can never be wholly produced, as that would require a respite, however short-lived; a recognition of a moment fixed in a past that is already beyond past. Instead, the image dissolves through gradations of colour and form, as endless a cycle as the passage of one season into the next (and into the next); and easily read as symbolic, encompassing the very processes of human existence, but through an articulation of knowledge that is experienced as pure sensation. Here, when I speak of the time-image as a cycle, I am thinking of Nietzsche's doctrine of eternal return where time functions as a circle that is not round. In this context, time is not eternal, because this would require a linearity that does not exist in the affective plane (Rodowick, 132). This is the crystalline regime in its truest expression, what Deleuze would depict as plunging into time, rather than crossing space.

Returning to the film, as the title card drops away we discover that the strains of "My Favorite Things" cited earlier are being played on an old upright piano at a church-basement rehearsal for a small-town production of *The Sound of Music*. A subtitle reads: Washington State, 1964. It is also here that we have our first introduction to Selma, the "ethereal sprite whose plaintive voice can break your heart," (Matthews) though a man involved in the show expresses disappointment at her having been cast in the lead role, because he thinks she "sings funny" and finds her dancing "not all that great either." But such is the nature of Selma, a woman of clearly humble origins whose perceived fragility is actually just a manifestation of an utter lack of pretension, a quality that she *inherits* from her portrayer. And though we might choose to remain distanced from this line of discourse, it is impossible to completely ignore the intertextual resonance of Björk in the role.[48] For the autodidactic nature of Björk's iconoclastic performance parallels that of Emily Watson's in its transcendent honesty, "inventing a new style of acting, if not an entirely new kind of human being" (Scott). And it would seem that Björk uncovers Selma's fundamental qualities through an instinctual process which requires her to really just play herself.

Here, within the organic regime, we can also identify a cross-textual recollection-sound in those moments when we hear Selma's voice in song. Yet this does not pose too much of a quandary as the culturally-literate spectator who comprises the bulk of von Trier's audience, at least in North America, participates in an extended disavowal that enables them to read the character without excessive distraction. That said, this line of thinking returns us to a psychoanalytic approach that has already been tagged as problematic. Instead, we might think the recollection-image not as an agent of memory, but rather, of *fabulation* – what Rodowick describes as a "collective enunciation" (156). For as Deleuze and Guattari assert, "we write not with childhood memories, but through blocs of childhood that are the becoming-child of the present" (Deleuze and Guattari, 1994: 168). And so with *Dancer in the*

Dark, where the degree of artifice built into the generic tropes organizes the diegesis, not to mention the purposely vague American setting and its international cast who make little effort to disguise their accents, we are able to move beyond the precincts of intertext and its hermeneutical methodology. In doing so, we discover that this fabulation – in which the body becomes another through "an act of story-telling that connects [it] to a people past or to come" (Deleuze, 1989: 275) – can be best read as a creative process that enriches rather than corrodes: Selma's "guileless, faltering vulnerability" (Scott) fortified by Björk's "vibrant humanity" (Travers).

But though we see evidence of this vibrancy and determination in Selma's efforts to master the song and dance routines choreographed by the musical-within-a-musical's director, her true resolve is revealed to a greater extent in the following scene, when we first discover that she is losing her eyesight. Knowing that she must keep her job at the factory in order to save money and protect her son Gene from suffering this misfortune, Selma shrewdly memorizes the eye chart so that the optometrist[49] can in good conscience recommend her continued employment. It is in the following scene, however, that we discover that it is not just this encroaching blindness, nor difficulties with the wayward Gene,[50] that have elicited comments and concerns from her supervisor. Rather, it is the hovering insistence of the *always-already* present masochistic plane – the regime of the crystalline, whose affective power is channelled through the prism of the time-image[51] – which constantly challenges Selma's capacity to remain focused on the task at hand.

For in this film, the composition of the bipartite text has taken on an entirely new appearance, different from that of *Breaking the Waves* with its checkerboard structure alternating between the narrative sequences and the time-images. Here, the masochistic plane shadows the narrative, always present as though hovering on the periphery, but only entering into the organic body in those moments when Selma gives it license to do so. It extends itself as though with fingers, reaching down and plucking Selma from the muck of her existence and shaking her free of its residue – if only fleetingly. For Selma is a daydreamer. Caught up in the realm of the imagination epitomized by Hollywood's classical cinema and its fairytale expressions of happiness, monetary success, and the American Dream, she yearns to escape from the pressures of her admittedly punishing life by travelling across the textual boundary to a place where she believes that "nothing dreadful ever happens." But *Dancer in the Dark* is not an example of the rags-to-riches stories perpetuated by the films that she loves so dearly.

Instead, it is a tragic chronicle of misguided faith, its narrative driven toward its brutal conclusion by the metaphorical and literal blindness of a mother's unconditional love.

Around the time of the Second World War – the very same era that would bear witness to the transformation of the cinematic image from one primarily of movement, to one focused on time – what we have come to know as the musical was born in America. These "pure entertainments" (Dyer, 176) offered audiences a respite from the bleak realities of the depression years, and the very real engagement of a nation at war, through the creation of fantastic technicolour worlds filled with handsome couples, beautiful vistas and happy endings, all conveyed through music and dance. Despite its escapist nature, however, the genre in its original state did not "present models of utopian worlds" as the more explicitly futuristic science fiction films of the 1950s would do a decade later. Rather, theirs was a utopianism "contained in the feelings it embodies... the sense that things could be better, that something other than what is [could] be imagined and maybe realised" (Dyer, 177). Richard Dyer's use of the word "entertainment" to describe these films is significant here, as in the critical response generated by *Dancer in the Dark*, what many reviewers have found most objectionable is that the film is by all appearances a *musical*, yet is neither "well made... in good taste" nor "plausible or entertaining" (Ebert). But what does the word *entertainment* actually mean in this particular context?

In the preface to Dyer's article, Rick Altman investigates its etymology and reaches some interesting conclusions. He finds that in its earliest English usage, it was "borrowed" from the French verb *entretenir* (to converse about), indicating a "discursive phenomenon rather than an impersonal narrative form. Let me entertain you = Let me hold your interest," whereas in practice, the French use the verb *divertir* to describe such amusements. This makes sense, as we often refer to entertainments as diversions (Dyer, 1975). Looking in the English dictionary for *diversion*, we find a definition that seems to fit: a "recreation or pastime... [for] diverting the mind from preoccupation or boredom" (Barber, 406). And so a critique that accuses von Trier of being "staggeringly insensitive to the values of the film musical" (Arroyo) seems to somewhat angrily miss the point. This is telling, for in truth, *Dancer in the Dark* is a film that *entertains* in both definitions of the term, and so is perhaps not insensate to the genre, but rather has created, in its unique bipartite structure, what might be argued as the quintessence of the musical form. For though its narrative sequences are often painful to watch, the repeated intrusions of the masochistic regime divert our attention away from the tribulations of the organic, plunging us into a "dreamy lapse [where we experience] not joy and sorrow perhaps, but the poignancy of both" (Dyer).[52]

Back at the factory, we experience one of these *intrusions* for the first time. As Selma's body numbly executes the repetitive gestures required by the apparatus of the metal press, removing kitchen sinks as quickly as they are released by its mechanical arms, her voice – which must not be confused with speech, for it is simply the medium, the object (Chion, 1999: 1) – participates in what we might describe as a corporeal and textual betrayal, alerting us to this alternate space-time that is always ever-present. In what I have earlier described as a transtextual dialogue, Selma sings along with a music that is not present in the diegesis, though the factory colludes in the building of this fantasy: the "clatter, crash, clack" of the active machines transforming these *territory sounds* – those auditory vibrations that identify a "particular locale through their pervasive and continuous presence" (Chion, 1995: 75) – into a rhythmic musicality. As is the case in many films, *Dancer in the Dark* passes "subtly from organic to crystalline images or combin[es] them in various ways" (Rodowick, 91) through this *reaching into* the plane of the narrative by the masochistic regime. This causes incommensurable thought to rise to the surface, for both Selma and the viewer, as the time-sound battles against the sadistic trajectory of the movement-sound's causal chain. But despite Selma's desire to enter into full communion with this world outside the diegesis, she is not yet ready, her voice reaches toward the crystalline, but the lyrics keep her clearly rooted in the organic. And so the narrative reasserts itself upon the fantastic, and Selma, bolstered by her love for Gene and her need to save money for the costly medical procedure, resigns herself to its stipulations and returns to what we might identify – in the absence of a less problematic term – as reality.

But reality is not at all kind to Selma, nor to Gene. As she repeatedly states, she is "not one of those moms" who can provide her son with material rewards, but though this is to some extent true – she is an impoverished single mother, dependent on a low-paying factory job and the kindness of Bill and Linda, who allow her and Gene to live in a trailer in their backyard – it is mostly just part of the elaborate ruse she maintains so that Gene will not discover that he too is at risk for blindness. For though we have little backstory when it comes to the film's characters, we do know something of Selma and her history: she was born in Communist Czechoslovakia, and has a fictional father who she pretends to send money to every month – money that she instead stashes away in a small tin, saving for

Gene's thirteenth birthday when he will be old enough to have the much-anticipated operation to restore his as yet unobstructed vision.

In many ways, Selma is engaged in a mental process that we might describe as a sort of *productive* amnesia.[53] As Deleuze contemplates in his discussion of Welles' films: how does a character "make *one's own* past incapable of being recalled?" (1989: 113). The response: amnesia. For Selma – whose past existence has been washed away by geographic displacement and the hardships of an immigrant's life – it is the amnesiac's disconnect with history that allows her to produce the idea of her father as a Czech tap-dancing legend. By consciously refusing to acknowledge those truths which are outside of desire, Selma seeks to maintain a worldview made manifest by this desire: optimistic, passionate, determined, and courageous. But as it was with Sade's *Justine*, in the work of suppressing these recollections, (Deleuze, 1989: 113) repression has become Selma's whole being: "repression of sex, of anger, of her own violence" (Carter, 48). And so she is made even more vulnerable to the lure of the masochistic text when it appears on the horizon and draws her into its swirling eddy. These notions of memory and recollection are also fundamental to our reading of *Dancer in the Dark*'s conclusive moments, and so it is essential to include a preliminary mediation on the subject here.

Memory is a truly fascinating contrivance. When thinking about memory, we must first remember that there is no conception of memory that exists outside of temporality as what we have come to understand by this concept – the recollection of past events captured and preserved in the present that was, and ready to be recalled and relived indefinitely – is in actuality an elaborate fiction, an impossibility. For in life, as it is with movement, everything is always already transformed. Collectively, as a society, and as individuals, we may strive to return to things: a safer time, an era of peace, or freedom, or security. But in truth, there is effectively nothing to return to because the past must always be read through the lens of the future, and so can never be anything more than a semblance of what it was. In this new space-time, there may be reverberations of the past that was, but these are merely echoes, transformed by the future that has not yet occurred before they can be created in the present. As Nietzsche states, "the present must coexist with itself as past and yet to come" (Deleuze, 1983: 48). This is the only present – the only possible truth.

In the same vein, the cinematic can "never be reduced to a simple unity, nor can the relation between image and thought be reduced to a simple, punctual present" (Rodowick, 8).

54

As we interact with the text, it is transformed by who we are in that moment, and more importantly, by who we are to become. Here, I am reminded of something Godard once said at a film festival Q&A when asked why he had decided to screen a particular film in one of their "influences" programs. Having not set his words to paper, I can only give an account of what I remember – an already sticky proposition. In effect, what he said was that there is no such thing as a text that can be understood as having influenced a body of work; that the film he had chosen was simply one that he had engaged with on a particular day, at a particular time, and that he had been moved by in that moment. What this suggests is that you can never go back and re-watch a cinematic text or re-read a book, and re-experience the phenomenon of that primary engagement in exactly the same way. This is also true for Selma, but on a very explicit, sensorial level, because for her, memory is contained in that which no longer exists, her encroaching blindness making the world *always-already* changed – less clear than it was the day before, and impossible to reconcile with what will come tomorrow. And so, as we encounter the textual body, even one that we have engaged with in the past, we must be clear that our engagement is one of *reading* or *watching* or *listening* – made unique by the very nature of the space-time in which it is encountered anew. This is the process that Deleuze illuminates when he introduces the concept of fabulation – or at the very least, is an appropriation of Deleuze's concept, transformed by need and fashioned anew as a framework for thinking about the recollection-image and memory.

As mentioned earlier, fabulation can be understood mostly straightforwardly (and in linguistic translation) as the practice of story-telling. In a strict Deleuzian sense, it is a mode of discourse that engenders minority voices, "where I becomes other and others can begin to become in recognition of a collectively elaborated I" (Rodowick, 156) – this is the body politic as becoming. That said, having articulated my approach to this thesis as one that is able to diverge from Deleuze, and thereby create new concepts, I seek a new modality of fabulation here – one that is grounded in Deleuze's philosophy, but is at the same time, liberated from the specificities of his project. For the most part, what I seek is a way to talk about memory that fully acknowledges what is most problematic: that memory, in its everyday conception, does not exist. But, if memory is indeed an impossibility, then how do we come to terms with the recollection-image? The easiest way to grapple with this apparent contradiction is to return to Deleuze's typology: for the recollection-image is a time-image, and in the time-image there is no such thing as linearity. And so we return to fabulation, a practice that is "performative in the philosophical as well as the theatrical sense... [and] inseparable from the time of enunciation... neither document nor work of fiction, but a form of enunciation that gravitates between these poles" (Rodowick, 157). But where does this knowledge ultimately leave us?

In the previous chapters, I have argued that we locate our suffering in the *any-space-whatever* that exists between the relational planes of this new sado-masochistic construct, because it is there that we are made vulnerable by the time-image's affective power, and from there that we are thrust back into the emotionally brutalizing trajectory of the movement-image. Taking this supposition one step further, fabulation (which we understand as external to narration) must be recognized as a function of the crystalline regime. Because of this, we can argue that in the bipartite structure of von Trier's films, when the sadistic text ruptures the affective space, it shatters the moment of fabulation as well, leaving us alienated and anomic, orphaned from ourselves – disconnected from the writing of a collective history which might otherwise have offered some *protection*. The recollection-image (and sound) is our salvation. Conceptualized now as an agent of writing rather than memory, we can enunciate the recollection-image as one that draws from a vast repository of images across space and time, thereby writing a pristine image that in this moment both resembles, and is greater than, the one that existed before.

Leaving this discussion aside for the moment, however, we must return to the film, and to the first active engagement of the masochistic text. Realizing that her sight is vanishing more quickly than she had expected, Selma asks for extra shifts at the factory, praying that she will be able to earn enough money before the owner realizes that she has been lying about her condition. And it is here, when the causality of the narrative becomes too much for her to bear, and the lure of the machines' mechanized cadences are too tantalizing to ignore, that she summons her courage and moves into the crystalline – slipping into its rhythms, which are then transformed through an audio dissolve to the more fully orchestrated music that provides the backing track for this first song and dance sequence. Now, the repeated chug and whir of the press is able to rise above its everyday function, serving as a "bridge between [the] time-bound narrative and the timeless transcendence of supra-diegetic music" (Altman, 1987: 67) – a term that is used by Altman in an attempt to reach toward that property of the musical which is otherwise so difficult to name: the intrinsic transtextuality that demands a more versatile articulation of diegetic space.

The scene begins with an affection-image, a close-up of Selma, who escapes certain catastrophe when Cvalda notices that she has put one too many steel plates into the press. With eyes closed, Selma allows her other senses to fully take over. A knowing smile, the action-image, indicates that the transformation has begun. Here, the sounds are not consumed by instrumentation but remain true to their source, yet a different musicality is created as they are cropped and made syncopated by the orchestration. It is also important to note that here too is the moment from which we take our cue, giving ourselves over to the time-image with a sensorial response that does not replace conscious thought, but certainly transcends its limits. Selma joins in the chorus, giving names to each of these new sounds, and using them to write her story. This first interlude is a tribute to Cvalda, who is not only Selma's closest confidante, but her eyes as well. Selma thinks Cvalda, who is very much a body-*with*-organs, is too serious, and beckons her to move beyond her organs and dance, entering into this world of the time-sound. But though Cvalda agrees to enter, she is very much the reluctant participant, frowning and rolling her eyes as she tries in vain to return to her work.

Here, colours are transformed in the mise-en-scène, gaining in intensity and tone so that they resemble the technicolour hues of the classic Hollywood musicals. But that is where the similarities end. In fact, with its one hundred digital cameras shooting from all corners of the set, the fantasy plays out like a "Busby Berkeley number passed under the blade of a Benihana chef... [ending in] a bewildering hash" (Edelstein). As in a scene out of Eisenstein or Pudovkin – in the use of a fragmented and formalist montage, the industrial setting and revolutionary tone – the factory's workers embrace the chance to be set free, as though from shackles, and abandoning their posts, take up the cause. In this *any-space-whatever*, Cvalda eventually begins to dance, won over by the joyous abandon of Selma's fantasy where the machines continue to pump forward, maintaining their productivity even as their operators succumb to the entrancing rhythms. But such elation is not to last, as the sudden appearance of a movement-image, faded and coarse, inserts itself into the masochistic realm, and we see Selma's oblivious face as the press grinds to a screeching halt, and her fellow employees rush over to see the damage that has been done. As a result, the factory is forced to stop production for the day, leaving Selma's future employment even more uncertain.

This crashing in of the sadistic text aggressively shatters generic expectations as the song and dance sequences of traditional musicals work to move the story toward its glorious conclusions. Such films do return their characters (and the audience) to the "real" world of the narrative at the end of each lyrical number, but do so knowing that this world has been made just a little bit better than it was before: more beautiful, more optimistic, more honest, more liberated. As Selma quite rightly maintains throughout the film, the world of the musical is supposed to comprise a "utopian space where suffering is abolished," (Matthews) but as the sadistic text reasserts its dominion again and again, it becomes painfully obvious that this is not going to be the case here. And so while it is certainly true that a "woman's possible utopian gaze may transcend her own image… if she becomes an active spectator in her own right… and if she succeeds in holding her own ground," (Gleber, 76) Selma is ultimately as powerless as Bess when it comes to making a full escape from the brutal demonstrations of the sadistic regime. For despite her ability to call forth the musical text as a body beckons the dream world by entering into a contract with sleep, and her dexterity as a lucid dreamer – who knows that she is asleep and so can fully partake in the dream world's disavowals – Selma lacks the ability to control either the outcome or the duration of these musical events. Consequently, though she has the capacity for freeing up "her own gaze onto an exterior world of new sights and views, " (Gleber, 76) this world exists only on the fringes, in the peripheral audio-vision of the newly sightless, and so remains firmly out of her grasp, serving only to restate and re-emphasize the dystopian character of the organic plane.

Yet despite this subjection, Selma (like Bess before her) has been graced with an ability to believe that transcendence is possible, that she will enter the modern, despite the many indications that the truth lies elsewhere. But hers is not a religious conviction. Rather, she is sustained by a faith in her own dedication and loyalty, in her capacity for hard work, and in her facility for tolerating the manifold deprivations that characterize her existence, whether monetary, romantic, or most significantly, optical. But this solid doggedness is also driven by a very tangible, enduring guilt. For Selma has a secret that few people have been made privy to: that she gave birth to Gene knowing full well that her condition was hereditary. And so she must not only live with this painful knowledge, but work even harder to right the wrongs of this selfish act. To summarize, this is a film about a woman who is losing her sight, and who is categorically traumatized by the fact that her son will one day lose his. As a result of this unspeakable burden and gnawing anxiety, Selma takes advantage of every resource at her disposal, working to the point of exhaustion to ensure the success of Gene's precious operation. And as it was with Bess in *Breaking the Waves*, Selma too is described by critics as the very "embodiment of selfless, innocent goodness," (Scott) but she is not completely without self-interest. For like Bess, who wants Jan to survive as much for herself as for him, Selma's sacrifice is motivated by the hope that in saving her son, she will achieve some redemption and be alleviated of the guilt which has led to her martyrdom. But what does this say about her character in the context of the pathologies discussed earlier?

Returning to Freud's classifications, it is easy to perceive Selma as exhibiting behaviours that could be read as morally masochistic, because for her "the suffering is enough," (165) it is "a thing-in-itself, perceived as part of her condition," (Carter, 52) though she subverts this suffering through a spiritual union with a world of pure fantasy. We could also designate her as a masochistic body in the Deleuzian articulation, because in the process of losing her vision, she is quite literally a body whose organs are caught up in a state of upheaval and transformation. Needless to say, we are each of us born a sensing body whose faculties develop and strengthen as we grow and age, to the point where they reach their apex, and begin to decline. We cannot arrest this process, but with advances in medical technology, we can sometimes slow it down. With Selma, however, we have the occasion to witness this progression in accelerated time, as her ability to fully sense is in sharp decline as the film begins. Because of this degeneration, Selma's other senses have been forced to engage in a struggle of reassessment and readjustment – an incontrovertible truth that is skilfully foreshadowed by the crystalline images of the opening sequence. And so Selma becomes the most explicit example of the BwO. Her body is never in stasis, never in rest. When she is in denial, when she implores her friends to ignore what is happening to her, she is fighting against the BwO – but this is a battle she cannot win, as the BwO is "already underway the moment the body has had enough of organs and wants to slough them off" (Deleuze and Guattari, 1987: 150).

It is also important to investigate Selma through the prism of the sadistic text, though this film is less faithful to its literary antecedents than was *Breaking the Waves*. On the whole, *Dancer in the Dark* is not as reiterative a text, nor is there much in the way of demonstration, that is, until the second half, which "moves through the stations of [Selma's] martyrdom like a medieval pageant" in which every moment contains the possibility of "suffering, humiliation or betrayal" (Scott). Additionally, Selma finds an awkward fit with the construction of the Sadeian heroine as we have come to recognize her, for though she toils endlessly and with little reward, she is never sexually violated, and is never physically tortured in the moments leading up to her death. That said, she is repeatedly brutalized by the movement-images of the organic text, a suffering made no less vicious for being psychologically rather than physically manifest. But there is something else that marks the most salient distinction between Bess and Selma in this regard. In fact, there is something entirely new happening here in terms of this heroine and her relationship with the textual body that we did not see in the earlier film. For in *Breaking the Waves*, the time-images are only apparent to the audience, and not felt or experienced by anyone within the world of the diegesis.

In *Dancer in the Dark*, Selma is ascribed an agency that allows her to bridge the gap between Bess and *Dogville*'s Grace – a later incarnation of von Trier's heroine who in *her* cross-textual transformation moves beyond the "uncompromising emotional absolutism" of Bess and Selma (Smith) and redirects her story, turning the tables on her tormentors, and in this moment, righting the wrongs of their misguided social experiment. But unlike Bess, who has only the voice of God to comfort her in times of need, Selma seems able to call forth the masochistic text and move into it, to a place where she knows there will always be "someone to catch her when she falls." While Bess could be said to experience a respite from the narrative in the crystalline regime – it is ultimately her salvation, though she is never aware of this extra-diegetic *kindness* – Selma, as though through a sheer force of will, brings about the intrusions that rupture the diegesis and suspend the narrative's trajectory. In doing so, she enables the transformation of the movement-image into what she needs it to be: a time-image. The time-sound, through its mere arrival on the cinematic horizon, functions as the agent of this change.

A useful example of this transformative authority takes place in the scene on the train bridge. Set in Washington State, but filmed entirely in Scandinavia, the film reveals little of its surrounding environs, situating its exteriors predominantly in the yard outside of Bill and Linda's house, in the parking lot of the factory, and along the railroad tracks that connect these two poles of Selma's existence. Hence, the presence of industry is experienced more directly through the mise-en-bande, made explicit by the sound of massive trucks that rumble past the factory gates, and the trains which carry their heaps of lumber to the distant cities of the west coast. For as mentioned in the introduction, this is a film about *audio-vision*; about that which allows Selma to *see* despite the fact that she is by this point almost completely blind. And so we too are made privy to the experience of *hearing* life, when diegetic sounds seek to overwhelm the mise-en-bande and its voices, but are instead taken hostage and delivered to the crystalline.

Here, as it was in the factory, those same diegetic sounds – the distant echoes of a train's whistle and the metrical chug-chug of its wheels against the tracks – anticipate the arrival of this crystalline when they begin to mutate, growing in volume as they take on alternate rhythms and instrumentation. Without hesitation, Selma greets these time-sounds by removing her glasses and tossing them into the river, a striking gesture that reveals a simple truth: she no longer needs them. With her audio-vision thus engaged, she tips her head and looks to the sky, making that which was previously imperceptible manifest, and in doing so, staking her claim on this newly discernible visible – what can be understood as a sort of visualized audible. In the narrative text, Selma's would-be-lover has followed her onto this bridge, worried about her ability to take care of herself, and determined that she acknowledge her loss of vision and seek interventions to reverse its course. But sadly, Selma has no patience for Jeff, her ever-present suitor, waiting at the factory gates with his ubiquitous offer of a ride home. She declares that she does not even want a boyfriend because she is too busy, but in fact, it is her broken heart – a heart consumed by guilt and grief – that stands in the way of this relationship; her martyrdom as a sexual being already complete. Yet he persists, and with her arrival on the masochistic plane, is first welcomed and then transformed, becoming a character who in this instance is made truly voiced (and so newly visible). She sings to him, and he answers back in song – voices in transcendence, communicating beyond narrative.

In this moment, as her communion with the textual presence beyond the organic takes root, Selma engages in a process of creative fabulation that moves "beyond the perceptual states and affective transitions of the lived" to where she is able to both *see* and *become* (Deleuze and Guattari, 1994: 171) – a sensing body whose aural faculties have transcended the visual, writing that which cannot (and will never) be remembered, and seeing the world as *always-already* transformed. This is an imperative moment, and one that I will return to in my discussion, because it is precisely this *taking root* in the crystalline that ultimately enables Selma to locate her salvation in the masochistic text of the concluding scene's "Next to Last Song" – allowing the BwO to write a story that becomes without images, in the time-image of fabulation, amorphous and eternal. The organic regime may seek to impose its indignities on the body-*with*-organs, but the BwO is replete with "gaiety, ecstasy, and dance," (Deleuze and Guattari, 1987: 150) and though it is "*always-already* obsolete, has been obsolete an infinite number of times, and will be obsolete countless more – as many times as there are adaptations and inventions," (Massumi, 109) it will retain its recollections. This is the quintessence of the cinematic BwO, "swinging between the surfaces that stratify it and the plane that sets it free… [revealing] itself for what it is: connection of desires, conjunction of flows, continuum of intensities" (Deleuze and Guattari, 1987: 161).

As mentioned earlier, in the field of film sound theory there are ongoing efforts to conceptualize and christen not only those sounds which travel around the periphery of the frame, but the spaces they inhabit as well. Jim Buhler and David Neumeyer have appropriated the notion of the *fantastic* in their attempt to describe "the gap between what we hear and what we see" (Buhler, 76) – while Claudia Gorbman takes another tack, employing the equally functional *metadiegetic* to articulate the sphere in which a character is able to "take over part of the film's narration, [thereby making the viewer] privileged to read [the character's] musical thoughts" (77). And then there is Michel Chion, the grandmaster of film sound theory, whose contributions include (but are in no way limited to) the concept of the *proscenium*, an aural space "at remove from the visual field" where the instruments creating the music are not discernible, but "gain the spotlight… perceived in their singularity and isolation" as non-synchronous or non-diegetic sounds (1999: 3-4). Each of these articulations are reaching towards equivalent conclusions, and have stemmed from the same types of observations, yet there is none among them that reaches far enough. Skating across the surface of the cinema, they catalogue and describe, but fail to fully address that which resonates beneath.

That said, when thinking about sound in the cinema, it is hard to fully divorce oneself from perpetuating a dichotomic approach to this binary, especially when doing so seems to engender a better mapping out of the manifold sounds existent in the mise-en-bande. At the outset, this was certainly the case here. For in each of these films – *Breaking the Waves* and *Dancer in the Dark* – there is something intentional happening around this polemic, though each is distinct in the mode of transit that its cross-textual reverberations take. By revealing the source of every piece of orchestration through the use of close-ups – the mechanics of the sink press, the wheels of the train along the tracks, or later, the needle point of a record player as it scratches repeatedly against the paper centre – von Trier makes these moments of transit

62

unambiguously manifest. But is our understanding of these processes necessarily dependent on a specific enunciation of the diegesis and its precincts?

When endeavouring to articulate the chain of complementary dyads upon which this thesis is constructed, it was theoretically productive to employ the diegetic binary as a point of reference, but assigning labour to the activity of naming and categorizing is simply of no value here. For whether the sound is diegetic, non-diegetic, or somewhere in the variously named in-between is ultimately irrelevant to this project. Instead, it is essential to remain squarely focused on the time-sound, the movement-sound, and the manner in which the relationship between the two impacts the spectatorial experience. What I seek then is the freedom to employ the concepts of sound theory as warranted, but interchangeably, releasing them from the specificities that individual scholars have assigned in their own monographs, and allowing them to morph into their new forms.

Thus far we have discussed the manifold ways that *Dancer in the Dark* pushes against the conventions of the musical genre, but with its illustration of the extremes of physical suffering and psychological torment, its overt emotional subject matter, and a plot that is impossible "to take seriously on any level," (Ebert) the film has also been categorized by critics as an "embarrassing" and "florid" melodrama (Matthews, Scott) whose grotesque exaggeration of the genre's narrative tropes is read as blasphemous. This is particularly evident in the movement-sounds of the mise-en-bande. For as it was with *Breaking the Waves*, in the organic regime of *Dancer in the Dark* there seems to be an explicit refusal to make meaning through the inclusion of thematic music – a "musical element that is repeated... [picking up] narrative associations, which... infuse themselves into each new thematic statement" (Gorbman, 16).[54] But thematic development is not the only task of these traditional non-diegetic musical interludes. On the one hand, they act as narrative cues, guiding our attention to the struggles of particular characters and their relationships – our anticipation encouraged through the deployment of these musical motifs. Yet it is their emotive function that is of perhaps the greatest import here, as the traditional melodramatic model uses these musical cues to stir the spirit of man, causing desires to bloom, and tears to well – conducting our emotional response to the events being portrayed onscreen with judiciously positioned instrumental swells.

Because there is music during the opening sequence of the film, not to mention the various song and dance sequences that intersect the narrative, the total absence of non-diegetic music on a thematic level is at times even more deeply experienced. This is especially true in those moments when our spectatorial conditioning lends an air of aural expectation to the narrative proceedings. Gorbman argues that when you remove music from scenes whose "emotional content is not explicit… you risk confronting the audience with an image they may fail to intercept," (18) and certainly for early filmmakers, "music was their panacea for encouraging audience empathy" (Brown, 12).[55] But no such cure-all is employed in *Dancer in the Dark*. In fact, von Trier's risk-taking is one of the film's greatest strengths, and it is precisely his desire to subvert the rules of this generic game that makes the movement-images of the sadistic plane so "immediate [and] palpable" (Gorbman, 18). For in his resistance to the overtly signifying structures of conventional melodramatic texts, von Trier creates a new spectatorial position in which the image is experienced as sensation; in the presence of musical silence, the movement-image is confronted by a time-sound and transformed. And it is in this modality that we are first made privy to the union of Selma and Bill.

Late one night, Bill arrives at Selma's door, desperately needing to talk with her. This is the moment when we see the relationship between them begin to take shape; their alliance forged in a fear of loss, and in guilt. The camera moves between them in wide-shot, a perception-image that seeks to draw them together. Then, with a sudden cut – for all the transitions in the empathic plane of *Dancer in the Dark* are cuts – we land on Selma, in profile and in close-up. She removes her glasses, and what at first seems merely an (albeit meaningful) gesture of intimacy and friendship is revealed again as indicative of a sensorial shift on Selma's part. Because of this, our attention is drawn again to the mise-en-bande; the visual and aural acting in collusion to encircle us in the cosseted world of this informal confessional. The action-image, which pulls us back to see Selma comforting Bill, her hands resting upon his arm, provides a transition to the reverse confession. As Selma begins to tell her deepest secret, the camera returns to the affection-image, and with it, to the affection-sound.

As truly befits the sensing body, Selma experiences Bill's suffering to a degree that transcends empathy. We can see this on the surface of her skin, an instantaneous, tactile response that makes this moment somehow inappropriate – too intimate to have taken place between a man and a woman who is not his wife. Here too, in the affective moment, our experience is one of sensation, a "purely visual touch" dependent on our collective knowledge of past touchings and other textures, *exteroceptive*.[56] Deleuze and Guattari refer to this sensibility as *haptic* (Massumi, 158) – a term which they prefer to tactile because it "does not establish an opposition between two sense organs but rather invites the assumption that the eye itself may fulfill this non-optical function" (Deleuze and Guattari, 1987: 492). This visual touch, which Massumi also describes as a *synesthesia proper to vision*, (158) can also be used to elucidate an experience of the cinema which allows us to first recognize, and then feel, the textures found in video images that have been shot in low light conditions, and transferred to 35mm film – the visual *noise* which we might describe as comparable to film grain; a quality inherent to the medium which creates the sensation of movement across the surface of the screen, the appearance of small dancing particles held captive by magnetic forces. In close-up, these textures are even more pronounced, and so we see that the affection-image is doing its job again, leaving us vulnerable and exposed in these moments to the "pure locus of the possible" (Deleuze, 1986: 109) or in this case, to the locus of the horrible.

This is also one of the scenes where we become acutely aware of the *absences* across the mise-en-bande, because with no music to "mitigate the verbal silence" there is an even greater emphasis on the fact that nobody is speaking (Gorbman, 18). This is the third manifestation of the affection-sound, the diegetic silences that accompany the responsive face in close-up, felt most profoundly after Selma has shared her secret and confessed that Gene's illness is her fault. In the moments following, a deep tonal silence falls across the screen, and in this instance, we are plunged headlong into the interval. As the scene continues to cut back and forth between extreme close-ups of Selma and Bill, sometimes talking and sometimes not, we are destabilized, falling into this interval over and over again. We are also made vulnerable by our second category of affection-sound here, as theirs are the hushed voices that arrive as whispered secrets. For though we are conscious of their inherently dialogic nature, and of the existence of an onscreen listener rendered invisible by the temporary exclusivity of the close-up, their voices are resonant on the skin of the ear, "wandering along the surface [of the haptic space] – *at once inside and outside* [as though] seeking a place to settle" (Chion, 1999: 23). But even as these affection-sounds work to propel the organic text forward, disclosing the data needed to pivot the narrative – that Bill is broke, and that Selma has a stash of money saved to cover the cost of Gene's operation – and send it toward its inevitable conclusion, they remain the visualized voices of the affection-image.

Throughout this conversation, Linda watches from her window as though fearing the worst: a vision of betrayal, of bodies commingling in sexual ecstasy. But Bill is not in love with Selma, and has no desire to betray Linda. Rather he seeks to keep Linda safe, to shelter her from the shocking truth of his utter financial ruin, and it is this protective instinct and love that has driven him to the moment of desperation. In a sense, though, what has just transpired between Bill and Selma is more momentous that anything Linda might imagine, for the first draft of a contract has been written – an allegiance forged in the silences that exist between spoken words – that take supremacy over every other relationship in Selma's life. And so Bill and Selma promise to keep each other's secrets, and in doing so, fully establish their relationship as one that is contractually-delineated. Their agreement is unwritten, yet remains impervious to external criticism or revision, even under the direst of circumstances; for when the prosecuting attorney asks Selma to state why she killed Bill in what seems to be cold blood, she answers simply: "because he asked me to." This despite her knowledge that the truth – that he had pointed a gun at her and stolen her savings – would literally set her free.

The murder itself is a particularly gruesome affair made even more cruel by the complete absence of music on the mise-en-bande. With nothing to "smooth over natural human fears of darkness and silence" (Brown, 12) and no time-sounds to offer comfort, or understanding, or escape, we too are abandoned to the brutalities of the sadistic text, and the consequences are great. From start to finish, this narrative sequence is at least ten minutes in length, a duration made even more unbearable by the silences that hang between the characters, ripe with betrayal and disappointments. But these are not pure silences, as the vibrations of lived life are felt in every moment. That said, the mise-en-bande seems intentionally free of any external diversions, as though the world outside has ceased to exist. And so there are no avenues for escape, and no affection-sounds acting as portals into the masochistic realm. When the excruciating echoes of Selma's exorcizing howls encircle us, and the sickening thuds of the safety deposit box smashing again and again into Bill's skull work their way under our skin – they are more terrifying and unspeakable than images alone could convey.

That the initial shooting is accidental is all but forgotten by this point, yet our knowledge of Bill's complicity is never quite forgotten. And so when Selma, covered in blood splatters and wholly exhausted by the physical and emotional violence she has just endured, collapses into a desk chair, we respond in kind. In this, the terrorizing nature of the organic regime can be said to have succeeded on two levels: engendering an empathic response in the spectator, one that is emotionally and physically akin to that experienced by the character on screen, and at the same time, achieving what we might describe as a sort of "moral victory" over this same spectator. For as it is with Sade, whose readers "urge the spotless Justine, just this once, to soil her hands with crime, " (Carter, 53) von Trier is also triumphant, as we find ourselves rooting for Selma, hoping that she will do what is "right" and punish Bill for his transgressions against her. The masochistic regime seems in agreement here, as it asserts itself on the narrative; the previously mentioned scratch-scratch of the record needle hitting the paper centre, marking the moment of transition. In what it is easily one of the film's most tender and touching sequences, Selma dances a slow waltz with the deceased Bill, and is granted forgiveness by all of those who love her including Bill, Linda, and her son, Gene. As she sings "I just did what I had to do," we are reminded again of the Sadeian heroine, and of Bess – locating her goodness in simply doing what she was told, or as is the case here, just doing what needed to be done – knowing full well that "the victim is always morally superior to the master... [which] is the victim's ambivalent triumph" (Carter, 56). Yet as always, the chance for catharsis is frustrated again (Anderson) and Selma is woken from her reverie by the territory sound of a car door slamming somewhere offscreen.

As posited earlier, thus far it has been difficult to locate the relationship between Selma and Bill within the literature of Sade or Sacher-Masoch, at least without pushing against the boundaries of their respective definitions. Which begs the question – is there really any reason to do so? Yet this is precisely what the critical response to the film has sought to do in its attempts to validate or decry the film's existence.[57] To say that this critical response has been impassioned is to understate the case to an almost ridiculous degree, with critics striving to surpass each other as though in a race to produce the most outrageous commentary on a film which some have described as akin to "watching a kitten get dragged behind a car" (Anderson) or "flies having their wings pulled off under a microscope" (Taylor). In fact, though von Trier's work generally inspires fairly extreme reactions, the film has provoked reviewers more so than *Breaking the Waves*.

Here, a dissatisfaction with the overly-simplistic rendering of the narrative elicits, in some viewers, a feeling of greater intolerance toward the visual style. Aggravated by the vertiginous effect of von Trier's aggressive hand-held strategies, they draw from an equally aggressive lexicon, situating their collective frustration in the cinematography which "forces itself on characters and audiences alike... insist[ing] on our participation [and] repeatedly strong-arming viewers into a forced intimacy that compels interest without being either believable or persuasive" (Turan).[58] In fact, what these responses suggest is an anger at the way in which von Trier manipulates his audience, but again, as in the academic realm, the critical body has not come to terms with the workings of the mise-en-bande, other than to note that the film is a musical, and that its star is Björk. And so, without new understandings as to how or why they might have been influenced by this text, they fall into blatant misreadings and over-simplified moralizing. This is especially true when it comes to discussing the film's concluding scenes.

In the days before her execution, Selma is befriended by a kindly prison guard who tries to help her cope with the excruciating boredom of solitary confinement, but when she encourages Selma to imagine something positive, the suggestion falls on ears that have lost their ability to hear. For in the town's prison, there is only the drone of air circulating through the otherwise hermetic cell, an unchanging sonic landscape through which no transtextual opportunities are produced. What is made painfully clear in this scene is the fact that the sadistic text has gained total dominion over the masochistic, leaving Selma abandoned in a narrative completely devoid of territory sounds, the clicks and clacks which in the past have offered solace in times of struggle. For like Bess before her, in surrendering to the act of negation required to irrevocably give oneself over to an ideal – in this case, the belief that keeping a promise is more important than staying alive – Selma has moved into a state of resolved amnesia so absolute that she is incapable of recalling these sounds on her own, and so cannot engage in any acts of albeit temporary deliverance. She has lost the ability to remember, the capacity for fabulation. Here, the silence is truly unbearable, and though the images jump from cut to cut, the duration of the sound-image stretches out against linearity and falls into time.

Later, when distant strains of hymn singing filter through the ventilation system, Selma is optimistic and presses her ear against the grate, but fails to establish a rhythm within its monotonous tone. Desperate for release, she starts to sing in halting broken chunks, banging her toothbrush against the metal sink and jumping on the bed, but is never able to produce the structures upon which she can layer her voice. This is another remarkable scene because it concretizes our identification of Selma as the quintessential BwO. On the mise-en-bande, there is her voice, coarse with sobs, her weakened breath threatening to run with every phrase. Here, the normally emergent recollection-sound of her voice in song struggles to take hold, but cannot recover itself – it is too restrained, too choked and ragged to summon recollection. Instead, it remains a movement-sound, held fast in the sadistic regime and serving only to remind us of the hopelessness of her plight. The mise-en-scène colludes with its aural counterpart, as Selma is dismembered by the cut, her disembodied voice aching for recognition over close-up shots of hands, and feet, and torso, interspersed with inanimate objects such as sinks, and door frames, and bed posts. At the same time, there are multiple layers of histories gathering in the folds of "My Favourite Things," but as amnesia and muteness have made recollection impossible – for both Selma and the viewer – they too remain functions of the narrative regime.

The guard recognizes this transtextual failure and shows up to escort Selma to the execution in a pair of heavy-soled shoes, stomping her feet against the hard surface of the floor, and forcing the rhythms that she knows will enable Selma to make this final journey. Though sombre in tone, the song that accompanies these one hundred and seven steps is able to provide transcendent space-time for Selma, who steps away from the sadistic text, singing and dancing her way down the long hallway. Again, a slamming door is the action-image that returns us to the cold reality of the narrative regime.

But once inside the execution chamber, something extraordinary happens. The guard takes her place with the assembled crowd as the noose is dropped over Selma's head. Here, we see Selma in extreme close-up, and the silence that echoes in the unseen spaces surrounding her drops us into the interval created by the affection-sound. Then, with no transtextual provocation, she begins to sing, recovering her voice and in doing so, taking authority over the writing of her story. These too are affection-sounds, as they accompany the face in close-up, and like Selma, we too are soothed by the presence of this ongoing communion with the crystalline. And so, as the ringing of the bell in *Breaking the Waves* informed us that Bess had been freed from her corporeal internment and found solace in the time-sound, Selma too is granted a reprieve. For in these final moments, we witness Selma's agency to a degree not seen before, as she moves of her own volition beyond the space-time consigned by the diegesis. The lyrics now are hers, and hers alone, and as her voice grows in texture and clarity, the moment of fabulation becomes more resonant.

It had always been Selma's practice to leave the theatre just after the "next to last song" because in doing so, she would be able to carry the magic of the cinema into the outside world. With eyes closed, she knows where she is going and what it will take to get there. In this instance, her sightlessness becomes a *movement-vision* that "passes into the body and through it to another space... [so that the body is transformed, becoming instead] – a *body without an image*" (Massumi, 57). When the floor drops out from beneath her, the "present is lost with the missing half-second, [as though] too quickly... to have [actually] happened" (Massumi, 30). And in a sense this is true, for the *body without an image* has already departed, moving through the portal presented by the affection-sound into the time-sound of silence, long before the arrival of the movement-sound returns us to the horizon of the sadistic plane.

And so we have gained an understanding of what happens to Selma at the end of *Dancer in the Dark*, but what is it exactly that has happened to us? As Selma begins to sing the "Next to Last Song," the audience free-floats into the time-sound of Selma's voice in isolation, drawn into a reduced state of consciousness as though "hypnotized" (Björkman, quoting von Trier, 96). And so it comes as no surprise that the moment in which the noose snaps hits the viewer as though with a sledgehammer, coming as it does with the suddenness of an unexpected blow. The movement-sound shatters the moment of suspended fabulation, and hurtles us back into the narrative; transformed in this moment into bodies-*with*-organs, we experience this return to the sadistic plane with an overwhelming physicality. Then, before we have the chance to recover our sense of time and space, we are plunged into the inescapable interval of complete and utter silence; a silence that is only possible when cinema is reduced to a purely optical experience – as it is in the final moments of this film. As one critic asked: "Where else should a movie leave you? Why should you expect to be transported?" (Scott). But we are transported, it is just that our destination is a space-time that has been stripped of the power to comfort. For as Deleuze warns, when "you free [the BwO] with too violent an action... [and] blow apart the strata without taking precautions, then instead of drawing the plane, you will be killed, plunged into a black hole, or even dragged toward catastrophe" (Deleuze and Guattari, 1987: 161). But how can we best articulate this experience in terms of our discussion here – is this truly an experience of the senses, or is there something happening on a deeper level?

Brian Massumi's "The Bleed: Where Body Meets Image" proffers a constructive mode for approaching these questions. The solution lies in something he calls *viscerality*. This is a sensibility that resides "in a second dimension of the flesh: one that is deeper than the stratum of proprioception"[59] because it is farther from the surface of the skin (Massumi, 60). It is also a concept that can be understood as a "rupture... [or] leap in place into a space outside action-reaction circuits." The new space-time where the body lands, what I have called the *destination*, is one in which there is an "inability to act or reflect... so taut a receptivity that the body is paralyzed until it is jolted back into action-reaction by recognition" (Massumi, 61). The problem in *Dancer in the Dark*, is that there is no jolting back to the narrative, and no recognition – there is only suffering.

In any case, it was Coop who had found us that evening in the barn and had mistaken our identities, who had eventually come over to me and lifted me into his embrace and said, 'Claire, my god, Claire,' and I had thought, then I am not Anna, then that must be Anna over there.

- Michael Ondaatje

CONCLUSION

The End of Subjectivity

And so we have come to the end, and with this end, to the realization that what is over, what has been put to rest (or what must be put to rest) is the notion of the spectator as subject – of the spectatorial experience as one of emotional, subjective response. For nothing could be further from the truth. In fact, we can no longer "organize and classify our mechanisms of viewing and reception according to [any] known and tried methods: we must always watch for the first time" (Manning) – watch as bodies not in stasis, not held in a fixed moment of conscious recognition and response, but as bodies that move beyond subjectivity into the collectivity of becoming. This is the function of the gap, of the interval between the time-image and the movement-image, between the sadistic text and the masochistic text, between sound and silence. Now time must be understood as having "no singular or self-identified subject because we think, exist and live in time... [and so there is only] change, deterritorialization, repetition as difference, the singular becoming multiple" (Rodowick, 140). This is the place of fabulation, of non-conscious recollection, of intensity and *passion*,[60] of sensation and viscerality – of suffering.

And so we have arrived at the affective space, a space that exists beyond true and false. For as we come to terms with the relationship between the complementary planes of the binary-chain, and how this interplay of regimes produces the affective moment, we must acknowledge that it has nothing to do with that which we have come to understand as the *real*. As Ondaatje posits in his poetic and structurally innovative *Divisadero*,[61] even identity must be seen as transient and transformable: *then I am not Anna, then that must be Anna over there*. There is no *real*, there is only affect – the *virtual as point of view*, a synesthesia of perception (Massumi, 35). Like Bess and Selma before them, Claire and Anna must be understood as becoming bodies; BwOs who inhabit a space that exists, not only beyond true and false, but beyond good and evil as well – for the affective is a space outside of causality, outside of judgement. But unlike their literary counterparts, Bess and Selma inhabit a space that moves in three-dimensions, fleshed-out and humanized, voiced and empowered by the cinematic text. An important note: we must never recognize the acts of these women as masochistic – they are not. Instead, we must see them for what they are: heroines within the Sadeian text who are released as BwOs by the intrusions of the masochistic text – stretching out across the horizon of the film, as though standing by for further instruction; waiting on the periphery of the frame, ever-present and all-powerful.

As this thesis has attempted to illustrate, we too are made vulnerable by the films of Lars von Trier because of the ways in which his texts alternate between their organic and crystalline regimes. But is this not in some way true of every film? For the most part, the answer is yes. As Deleuze discusses in the two *Cinema* books, his project does not make a plea for one type of image over the other. The arrival of the time-image does not invalidate the contributions of the movement-image; one is not subordinate to the other. And in most contemporary narrative films, we see evidence of time-images interspersed with images of movement. In fact, this is so common that most viewers would not find the identification of these time-images distracting – we take them for granted, oblivious to their function or effect. So what is different here? What makes the work of this thesis important is not what it says about von Trier's work in isolation, but what it constructs as a model for approaching his work; a model whose application extends beyond von Trier, and at the same time, functions as a modality for challenging the critical response that his films have garnered in the years since *Breaking the Waves*. It is not that what I am doing here is totally new – it is not. But in looking at his films in this light, I am writing against a mode of critique grounded in more traditional psychoanalytic theories of the cinema – thinking that equates a film's *sadomasochism* with a notion of "the director as torturer" (Gormley, 12) – polemicized with overly simplistic renderings of von Trier's thematics, and what seems to be a desire to hold him responsible for the way he makes us *feel*.

Here, there is no need for questions of accountability. There is no discourse over identification and sympathy. No need to lay blame or make apologies for him. This is not about how von Trier exploits his female characters, and the women who embody them, nor is it about the emotions that his machinations provoke in us. This is not about whether he, or his films, are sadistic, or about whether we are exhibiting some essential form of masochism in our willingness or compulsion to engage with these texts. As mentioned throughout, the critical reception that has greeted both *Breaking the Waves* and *Dancer in the Dark* (as well as *Idioterne*, *Dogville*, and to some extent, *Mandalay*) is redolent of a particular brand of subjectivity: self-congratulatory and self-serving. Perhaps this can be justified: they are simply doing their job of explanation and recommendation. Still, there is something unproductive in critical and/or academic readings that, engendered by works of such affective power, seem oblivious to the films' inherent textual and *intertextual* potentialities.[62]

Yet there is suffering – both onscreen and off. And there is understanding, and compassion, and stark, recognizable emotions. For these are women we come to care for, whose pain and suffering we feel as harshly as though it was our own. This, as Haruki Murakami posits, is the power of empathy, and the power of the empathic text, regardless of how sadistic the means for engendering this emotional response may be. So there is suffering – but no *victims*, at least in the traditional sense of the term. For victims are not generally given respite from brutality, nor are they freed from their torments, from the burden of their organs. These are bodies-*with*-organs, full of longing and terror, outside of collectivity, and unable to open the door.

There is something else going on here as well – there is affect, the swirling eddy that sucks us out of this excruciating torrent of brutality and subjugation, that frees the body from its organs, holding it steady and safe in moments of heretofore unknown bliss. This new body expands into time, and into a space of fabulation where it is free to read and write and live anew. It reaches toward the BwO, that which is out of reach, but yet *always-already* reached – the organs independent, contingent, "no longer anything more than intensities that are produced" (Deleuze and Guattari, 1987: 164). And so in the end, we are reminded of that which makes bi-partite texts, such as those found in *Breaking the Waves* and *Dancer in the Dark*, so revelatory – that in the conception of this newly demarcated affective space which exist in the interval between these two textual regimes, they provide an experience of the cinema that is richer, more profound, and more devastating than those offered by films composed primarily of movement-images.

As the work of Brian Massumi in *Parables for the Virtual* suggests, there are no limits as to where thinking on sensation and affect may take us, extending far beyond the literary and cinematic, to encompass an endless body of *texts* – both literal and virtual.[63] Perhaps the most valuable concept that emerges from this thesis, in terms of where this project may lead me, is that of the *any-space-whatever*, for it is here, in this virtual space of transition and transformation, that the possibility for new approaches to understanding our engagement with the world truly lies. While it may seem too far-reaching to talk about an engagement with the world in its entirety, what is offered by this course of philosophical enquiry into the body and its sensorial and corporeal potentialities, is just that: a new way of approaching reality, virtuality, and their manifold surfaces and planes, that reaches towards all aspects of our engagement with modern existence. As Massumi states in the introduction to *Parables*, "when I think of my body and ask what it does to earn that name, two things stand out. It *moves*. It *feels*. In fact, it does both at the same time" (2002: 1). Our bodies move and feel, but they do not move and feel in isolation. And so these affective spaces take on greater resonance, for it is in these moments that the collectivity of sensing bodies fully emerges, creating new possibilities for thinking about not only the body in its individual state, but in its relationship with the collectivity. Here is where we find understanding. Here is where we find hope.

WORKS CITED

Altman, Rick, ed. Sound Theory/Sound Practice. New York: Routledge, 1992.
--------"The American Film Musical: Paradigmatic Structure and Mediatory Function."
   Genre: The Musical. Ed. Rick Altman. London: Routledge & Kegan Paul Ltd., 1981:
   197-207.

Anderson, Jason. "Singing in the Pain." Rev. *Dancer in the Dark*. Dir. Lars von Trier.
   Retrieved June 27, 2005. Eye Magazine. October 5, 2000.
   <http://www.eye.net/eye/issue/issue_10.05.00/film/dancerinthedark.html>

Arpe, Malene. "Going the Distance: Director Lars von Trier Rides the Waves of True Love."
   Rev. *Breaking the Waves*. Dir. Lars von Trier. Retrieved June 27, 2005. Eye
   Magazine. November 21, 1996.
   <http://www.eye.net/eye/issue/issue_11.21.96/film/breaking.html>

Arroyo, José. "How do you solve a problem like von Trier?" Sight and Sound 10:9
   (September, 2000): 14-16.

Barber, Katherine, ed. The Canadian Oxford Dictionary. Toronto: Oxford University Press,
   1998.

Barthes, Roland. "The Death of the Author." Retrieved July 18, 2005. Image, Music, Text.
   1977. <http://faculty.smu.edu/dfoster/theory/Barthes.htm>

Belzer, Thomas. "Lars von Trier: The Little Knight." Retrieved July 15, 2005. Senses of
   Cinema. <http:www.sensesofcinema.com/contents/directors/02/vontrier.html>

Björk. "Statement on Lars von Trier." Retrieved July 20, 2005. Camera Eye.
   <http://www.cinemaeye.com/more/435_0_10_0_C>

Björkman, Stig. Trier on von Trier. Trans. Neil Smith. New York: Faber & Faber Limited,
   2003.

Black Book Magazine. Interview with Lars von Trier and Paul Thomas Anderson. Received
   by email on March 1, 2004. Date and Issue unknown.

Breaking the Waves. Dir. Lars von Trier. Perf. Stellan Skarsgård, Emily Watson. Zentropa,
   1996.

Brown, Royal, S. Overtones and Undertones: Reading Film Music. Berkeley: University of
   California Press, 1994.

Buhler, Jim, and David Neumeyer. "Analytic and Interpretive Approaches to Film Music (I):
   Analysing the Music." Film Music Critical Approaches. Ed. J.K. Donnelly. New
   York: The Continuum International Publishing Group, Inc., 2001.

Buhler, Jim, Anahid Kassabian, David Neumeyer, and Robyn Stilwell. "A Panel Discussion on Film Sound/Film Music." Ed. Kyle Barnett. The Velvet Light Trap 51 (2003): 73-91.

Carter, Angela. "The Desecration of the Temple: The Life of Justine." Sadeian Women and the Ideology of Pornography. New York: Pantheon Books, 1988: 38-77.

Chion, Michel. Audio-Vision. Claudia Gorbman, ed. New York: Columbia University Press, 1994.

--------The Voice in Cinema. Claudia Gorbman, ed. New York: Columbia University Press, 1999.

Dancer in the Dark. Dir. Lars von Trier. Perf. Björk, Catherine Deneuve. Zentropa, 2000.

Deleuze, Gilles. Masochism: An Interpretation of Coldness and Cruelty. New York: George Brazillier, 1971.

-------- Nietzsche and Philosophy. Hugh Tomlinson, trans. New York: Columbia UP, 1983.

--------The Movement-Image. Hugh Tomlinson and Barbara Habberjam, trans. Minneapolis: University of Minnesota Press, 1986.

--------The Time-Image. Hugh Tomlinson and Barbara Habberjam, trans. Minneapolis: University of Minnesota Press, 1989.

Deleuze, Gilles and Félix Guattari. A Thousand Plateaus: Capitalism and Schizophrenia. Brian Massumi, trans. Minneapolis: University of Minnesota Press, 1987.

--------What is Philosophy? Hugh Tomlinson and Graham Burchell, trans. New York: Columbia University Press, 1994.

Dogville. Dir. Lars von Trier. Perf. Paul Bettany, Nicole Kidman. Zentropa, 2003.

Dyer, Richard. "Entertainment and Utopia." Genre: The Musical. Ed. Rick Altman. London: Routledge & Kegan Paul Ltd., 1981: 175-189.

Ebert, Roger. Rev. Dancer in the Dark. Dir. Lars von Trier. Retrieved June 27, 2005. The Chicago Sun Times. October 20, 2000.
<http://rogerebert.suntimes.com/apps/pbcs.dll/article?AID=/20001020/REVIEWS/10 200302/1023>

Edelstein, David. "Dancer in the Dark Stumbles Badly in its Attempt to Make Björk into a Saint." Rev. Dancer in the Dark. Dir. Lars von Trier. Retrieved June 27, 2005. Slate Magazine. September 29, 2000. <http://slate.msn.com/id/90528>

--------"Welcome to the Dollhouse." Rev. Dogville. Dir. Lars von Trier. Retrieved July 15, 2005. Slate Magazine. March 25, 2004. <http://slate.msn.com/id/2097817>

Eliot, T.S. "The Wasteland." The Norton Anthology of Modern Poetry: Second Edition. Ed. Richard Ellman and Robert O'Clair. New York: W.W. Norton and Company, 1988: 495.

Freud, Sigmund. "The Economic Problems of Masochism." (1924). The Standard Edition of the Complete Psychological Works of Sigmund Freud (19). Trans. James Strachey. London: Hogarth Press, 1955: 155-170.

Flaxman, Gregory, ed. The Brain is the Screen: Deleuze and the Philosophy of Cinema. Minneapolis & London: University of Minnesota Press, 2000.

Gleber, Anke. "Women on the Screens and Streets of Modernity: In Search of the Female Flaneur." The Art of Taking a Walk: Flanerie, Literature, and Film in Weimar Culture. Princeton, NJ: Princeton University Press, 1999: 55-84.

Gopnik, Adam. "Death of a Fish: The Passing of a Betta and the Making of a Child's Mind." The New Yorker (July 4, 2005): 42-47.

Gorbman, Claudia. Unheard Melodies: Narrative Film Music. Bloomington, Indiana: Indiana University Press, 1987.

Gormley, Paul. The New-Brutality Film: Race and Affect in Contemporary Hollywood Cinema. Bristol, UK: Intellect Books. 2005.

Izod, John. The Films of Nicolas Roeg: Myth and Mind. New York: St. Martin's Press, 1992:67-86

Kaufmann, Stanley. Rev. Breaking the Waves. The New Republic 215:24 (Dec. 9, 1996): 26-28.

Kelly, Richard. The Name of this Book is Dogme 95. London: Faber & Faber Limited, 2000.

Kennedy, Harlan. "Orbiting Sublimity." Film Comment 32:4. (July-August, 1996): 6-8.

Kerr, Sarah. "Sex and Longing." Rev. Breaking the Waves. Dir. Lars von Trier. Retrieved June 27, 2005. Slate Magazine. Nov 12, 1996. <http://slate.msn.com/id/3188>

Lastra, James. "Sound Theory." Sound Technology and the American Cinema. New York: Columbia University Press, 2001: 123-153.

Lumholdt, Jan. Lars von Trier: Interviews. Jackson: University Press of Mississippi, 2003.

Makarushka, Irena, S.M. "Transgressing Goodness in Breaking the Waves." Journal of Religion and Film 2:1 (April, 1998): 1-11. Retrieved on July 4, 2005. <http://www.unomaha.edu/jrf/breaking.htm>

Manning, Erin. "Sensing Bodies." January, 2006.

Massumi, Brian. Parables for the Virtual: Movement, Affect, Sensation. Durham & London: Duke University Press, 2002.

Matthews, Peter. Rev. *Dancer in the Dark*. Dir. Lars von Trier. Retrieved June 27, 2005.
Sight and Sound (October, 2000).

Murakami, Haruki. The Wind-Up Bird Chronicles. New York: Vintage Books, 1997: 239.

Ondaatje, Michael. Divisadero. Toronto: McClelland & Stewart, 2007: 20.

Page, Tim. "Parallel Play: A Lifetime of Restless Isolation Explained." The New Yorker
(August 20, 2007): 36-41.

Powell, Anna. Deleuze and Horror Film. Edinburgh: Edinburgh University Press, 2005.

Rodowick, D.N. Gilles Deleuze's Time Machine. Durham, North Carolina: Duke University
Press, 2003.

Rosenbaum, Jonathan. "Mixed Emotions." Rev. *Breaking the Waves*. Dir. Lars von Trier.
Retrieved June 27, 2005. The Chicago Reader. 1997.
<http://www.chicagoreader.com/movies/archives/1296/12066.html>

Scott, A.O. "*Dancer in the Dark*: Universe Without Happy Endings." Rev. *Dancer in the
Dark*. Dir. Lars von Trier. The New York Times. September 22, 2000.

Smith, Gavin. "Imitation of Life: An Interview with Lars von Trier." Film Comment 36:5
(September/October, 2000).

Stevenson, Jack. Lars von Trier. London: British Film Institute, 2002.

Studlar, Gaylyn. In the Realm of Pleasure: Von Sternberg, Dietrich, and the Masochistic
Aesthetic. New York: Columbia University Press, 1988.

Szalita, Alberta. "Some Thoughts on Empathy. The Eighteenth Annual Frieda Fromm-
Reichmann Memorial Lecture." Psychiatry 39:2 (May, 1976): 142-52.

Taylor, Charles. Rev. *Dogville*. Dir. Lars von Trier. Retrieved August 13, 2007. Salon
Magazine. March 26, 2004.
<http://www.dir.salon.com/story/ent/movies/reviews/2004/03/26/dogville/index.html?
pn=1>

Totaro, Donato. "Gilles Deleuze's Bergsonian Film Project." Retrieved March 20, 2007.
Offscreen. March 31, 1999.
<http://www.horschamp.qc.ca/9903/offscreen_essays/deleuze1.html>

Travers, Peter. Rev. *Dancer in the Dark*. Dir. Lars von Trier. Retrieved June 27, 2005.
Rolling Stone Magazine. September, 2000.
<http://www.rollingstone.com/reviews/movies/id/5947905?pageid=re.Reviews
MovieArchive&pageregion&afl=imdb>

Turan, Kenneth. Rev. *Breaking the Waves*. Dir. Lars von Trier. Retrieved June 27, 2005. The Los Angeles Times. November 20, 1996.
<http://www.calendarlive.com/movies/reviews/cl-movie961120-1.story>

Von Trier, Lars. "Director's Note – This Film is About *Good*." Screenplay of *Breaking the Waves*. London: Faber & Faber Limited: 1996.

Wilmington, Michael. Rev. *Dogville*. Dir. Lars von Trier. Retrieved June 27, 2005. The Chicago Tribune. April 9, 2004.
<http://www.metromix.chicagotribune.com/movies/mmx-040409-movies-review-mw-dogville.story>

Worringer, Wilhelm. Abstraction and Empathy. Trans. Michael Bullock. New York: International Universities Press, 1953.

Zacharek, Stephanie. "Lars von Trier is a mechanic, not an artist." Rev. *Dancer in the Dark*. Dir. Lars von Trier. Retrieved June 27, 2005. Salon Magazine. September 22, 2000.
<http://dir.salon.com/ent/movies/review/2000/09/22/trier_dancer/index.html?CP=IMD&DN=110>

END NOTES

[1] See Kaufmann, Kennedy.

[2] Of *Dancer in the Dark*.

[3] Appropriating Michel Chion's term – from the title of his book – though not necessarily his definition.

[4] *Idioterne*, the second film in the *Goldheart* trilogy, is not included in this project for the simple reason that its strict adherence to Dogme's proscription that "the sound must never be produced apart from the images" (Kelly, 227) necessarily excludes it from this analysis with its emphasis on sounds existing outside of the diegesis.

[5] See Deleuze and Guattari (1987).

[6] The lineage of this quote is actually much more complicated, and in many ways speaks to the challenging task of working with Deleuze, for Totaro is quoting Jeffrey Bell, who in turn is summarizing Reda Bensmaia's interpretation of Deleuze's appropriation and transformation of the concepts articulated by Pascal Augé.

[7] From *Trier on von Trier* (Björkman, 143).

[8] It is important to note that Deleuze's semiotics moves away from the semiology of Saussure with its desire to "define the cinematic sign by imposing a linguistic model from the outside" (Rodowick, 7). Instead it derives from Peirce – a "system of images and signs independent of language… [which] exists in its reaction to a *non-language-material* that it transforms" (Deleuze, 1989: 29). That it is relational is what makes it unique, focusing on the links between signs in space and time, rather than the linguistic significance of the signs themselves.

[9] See Wilhelm Worringer.

[10] See von Trier's *Dogville*, for example.

[11] Deleuze's frequent collaborator, and colleague at the University of Paris, though Deleuze himself described their relationship less as a collaboration, than as a "negotiation" *between* philosopher and non-philosopher (Translators' Introduction from *What is Philosophy?*, viii)

[12] Notably absent from this selection is *Idioterne* (1998) – for the reason described in note 4.

[13] Though this has not been explicitly stated, it appears that von Trier has abandoned this trilogy after *Mandalay* – which generated little critical and/or popular interest.

[14] See Anna Powell and Paul Gormley.

[15] In *Dancer in the Dark*, music that is created outside of the diegetic space (in post-production, for example) is often read as diegetic, because of its logical connection to persons or objects within the diegetic space – though it is not generated *naturally* during the production of the film.

[16] Although the growing presence of video-description – a technique in which the visual elements of the film are aurally "described" on a secondary sound track – suggests that the mise-en-bande may

already be moving toward a more autonomous state; a *blind* cinema as opposed to the "*deaf* cinema" of the pre-sound era (Chion, 1999: 8).

[17] I am unclear as to who coined the term *sound-image*, and so have not assigned credit. Later in this chapter I employ two additional uncredited terms: the *time-sound* and the *movement-sound*.

[18] In *Audio-Vision*, Chion questions whether an audible slice of sound makes a sound shot (43) – looking for ways to talk about film sound that builds bridges to the methods of visual film analysis.

[19] From this point forward, I will use the word narrative to describe the organic regime that is constructed from movement-images – knowing that this term would not be used in conjunction with a strict Deleuzian approach (which this is not).

[20] This statement acknowledges that the word "natural" is fraught with inconsistencies because a filmmaker may manipulate a scene so that sound-creating objects that may not "normally" occur are suddenly present. For example: a radio in a bathroom, or a musician playing in an otherwise empty field. This type of manipulation has been much-discussed in light of the Dogme manifesto.

[21] From this point forward, when speaking in general terms, the term movement-image should be understood to represent both the movement-image and the movement-sound. The same will be true later when I move into a discussion of the time-image and time-sound.

[22] The term plane as used here bears no relationship to that articulated by Deleuze and Guattari in *What is Philosophy?* By binary-chain I am referring to the series of dyadic complements that are linked together through their relational properties. The empathic plane makes up the bottom half of the chain while the affective sits above. They are complementary to each other but function in different ways, motivated by different intents. An illustration of this model can be found on page 29.

[23] For it is only *Dogville*'s Grace who escapes the fate of her besieged predecessors, eluding the replacement of a cinematic surrogate, and suffering further indignities in *Mandalay* (albeit in the body of another actress – Bryce Dallas Howard).

[24] Interviews with Emily Watson have proved difficult to track down, though her co-star, Stellan Skarsgård, who described her as "terror-stricken," went on to portray the *Breaking the Waves* set as "enormously fun and nurturing" and possessing the "best of Danish coziness" with a "feeling of love and warmth" (Arpe).

[25] What makes *Caché* so provocative is that it is ostensibly a thriller in which a wealthy middle-aged couple begin to receive videotapes in the mail; evidence that they are being watched by some anonymous yet threatening presence. As the story proceeds, the husband moves closer and closer to solving the mystery – as per the conventions of the genre – as we become aware of his past transgressions, and meet the young man who seems to be responsible, seeking revenge for his own father's suffering and death. In the final scene, we expect our suspicions to be confirmed, but instead are faced with a long shot of even longer duration in which nothing appears to be happening at all. Upon closer inspection, we see that this young man has arrived on the steps of a school and is speaking with the victim's own son, but as the action is set in the far upper left-hand corner of the screen, and there is no microphone recording the conversation, it is only by accident that we notice this is taking place. That said, this *knowledge* does little to further our *understanding* of the story or provide any resolution to the narrative.

[26] The date of publication for the original French version of *What is Philosophy?*

[27] A term Deleuze uses to describe the naturalism of Stroheim and Buñuel (1986: 125) though there are dozens of directors whose work is celebrated in the two *Cinema* books.

[28] From the lyrics to "In a Broken Dream" by Python Lee Jackson, with Rod Stewart on lead vocals. This song accompanies the title card which reads: Chapter Two – Life with Jan.

[29] For this is the true character of the masochistic exchange.

[30] Although it should be noted that the senses are not necessarily in opposition to language.

[31] That these fantasies "place the subject in a characteristically female situation… castrated, or copulated with" (Freud, *Economic Problem*, 162) is what led Freud to label this masochistic form as *feminine*.

[32] Though the majority of Sacher-Masoch's fiction does revolve around male heroes, and Deleuze's interpretation here is of *Venus in Furs* with its protagonist, Severin, and his despotic master, Wanda, there need not be a gender distinction between roles.

[33] All of the citations in this paragraph, and the one that follows, if not named are from Deleuze's *Masochism*. Italicized terms are drawn directly from the referenced summary.

[34] The citations in this section find their source in the psychoanalysis of Theodore Reik who Deleuze feels deserves "special credit" for his work distinguishing four characteristics of masochism: fantasy, suspense, persuasion (demonstration), and provocation. From *Masochism in Sex and Society*. Trans. MH Beigel and GM Kurth. Grove Press, 1962: 44-91.

[35] I am uncertain as to who coined the phrase "masochistic aesthetic," but I acquired it from Gaylyn Studlar's *In The Realm of Pleasure*.

[36] As understood in Angela Carter's work on *The Life of Justine*.

[37] And as Deleuze and Guattari confirm, because "psychoanalysis translates everything into phantasies… it royally botches the real, because it botches the DwO" (1987, 151).

[38] In Gleber's article she quotes letters written by women at the time, unhappy with having someone else decide what museum they should go to, and how long they were allowed to spend with a particular piece.

[39] Carter's quote actually reads "she *is* fucked" because Justine has never had consensual sex and so locates her goodness in the fact that she "does not fuck" except when raped.

[40] For though we may argue against the notion of vococentrism in the cinema as a whole, we can acknowledge that in the organic regime of the narrative, the mise-en-bande can be seen as vococentric.

[41] As well as Deleuze and Guattari's *Anti-Oedipus*, and Artaud's work, from which it stems.

[42] Again, from Theodore Reik.

[43] There are a few examples of this throughout the film: the music at the wedding dance, the T-Rex song which accompanies the "Jan moves in" sequence (which seems non-diegetic until its source is revealed), as well as the examples referenced later in this chapter.

[44] In a sense we can recognize in Jan a version of Freud's second type of masochism: the feminine. For though Jan does not want to be treated as a "naughty child," he seeks to experience that which cannot be experienced through fantasy alone.

[45] From Langer's *Feeling and Form*.

[46] Such as the creaking of walls or the hum of a furnace; anything that cannot be turned off or controlled during the recording of the dialogue.

[47] Though a coda is by definition " the concluding passage in a piece or movement," it is the notion of a coda as something which is outside of, or "in addition to the basic structure" (Barber, 274) of the work that I appropriate here.

[48] Not to mention Catherine Deneuve as Cvalda.

[49] As played by Stellan Skarsgård, or Jan, from *Breaking the Waves*, the optometrist is an equally interesting recollection-image, but one best left to another project.

[50] An intentional pun, perhaps. As the "wayward Gene" refers both to the inherited traits which are causing Gene to go blind, and his proclivity for hanging around with the wrong crowd.

[51] As opposed to the sadistic plane, which I have identified as the organic regime of the narrative text, a text that is constructed primarily from movement-images.

[52] Again, quoting Langer.

[53] Productive in that it produces a new reality through its creation of the past.

[54] And it is the rejection of this generic norm which makes these films companions to those produced under the prescriptions of the *Dogme* manifesto – despite their many divergences from the Vows of Chastity.

[55] Brown is quoting Irwin Bazelon, from *Knowing the Score: Notes on Film Music* (New York: Van Nostrand Reinhold) 1975.

[56] Massumi uses the term exteroceptive to describe what he refers to as a tactile sensibility, and to distinguish this sensibility from that of the visceral, or interoceptive.

[57] For example, Stephanie Zacharek of *Salon.com* describes the movie as a "meat grinder" and accuses von Trier of showing "unabashed sadism toward his characters" and a delight for "making *us* suffer;" while A.O Scott of The *New York Times* calls the film one of the "most sadistic he has ever seen."

[58] The point is well taken. In fact, for a skilled cinematographer to create images that are as nausea-inducing as the ones beheld here, he must be extremely committed to doing just that. For even a student filmmaker, or a father at a birthday party – as long as they suffer from no nervous disorders – can produce a more stable image.

^{59} For Massumi, proprioception is a "sensibility proper to the muscles and ligaments… a dimension of the flesh… between skin and viscera" (58-59).

^{60} A term Massumi borrows from Steven Shaviro to describe the moment of *spasmodic passivity* and *paralysis* that occurs as a response to viscerality (61).

^{61} In Ondaatje's book, the initial narrative, in which the characters of Anna and Claire are introduced, is abandoned mid-way, upending the reader's expectations in terms of plot and character.

^{62} Here, again, it must be stressed that in my use of the term *intertextual*, I am referring to the affective space existent *between* the sadistic and masochistic planes, rather than the more traditional relationship between texts that is the basis of work in intertextuality and interdisciplinarity.

^{63} In my thinking here, a text can be anything – anything that can be *read*.

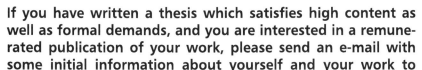

Printed in Great Britain
by Amazon.co.uk, Ltd.,
Marston Gate.